LIZ CHAMPION

Cake, anyone?

Scenes from everyday life in extraordinary times

Wells PRESS

First published by Wells Press 2020

Copyright © 2020 by Liz Champion

This book is a work of nonfiction based on the life of the author. Permission has been sought from the main characters featured in it.

Author image by Leyla Brooke – The Story of You.

First edition

ISBN: 978-1-8383028-0-1

Illustration by Glenda Strong
Cover art by Sarah Gough, G. Creative

This book was professionally typeset on Reedsy.
Find out more at reedsy.com

For Olivia

Contents

III   THE NEW NORMAL

Introduction

Hello, and welcome to *Cake, anyone? Scenes from everyday life in extraordinary times.*

And these are certainly extraordinary times — 2020 is a year that has changed everything and everyone.

At the start of the year, I was craving change (be careful what you wish for). On New Year's Eve, I welcomed in the new year with my husband, Chris. We were sitting in our car at the stables, making sure a midnight firework didn't set the whole yard ablaze (it's happened before, but that's another story). I vowed that 2020 was going to be different.

After years of studying and striving and working, I'd never had time to prioritise my writing and achieve my writing dreams. It was time to at least try. We'd also put our house on the market, so there was the exciting prospect of a new home. And, after turning forty in 2019, I was determined to make my forties a decade of fun. Life was going to become a big party. I had plans to travel and see the world, throwing myself into a life of Fun with a capital F.

Things started well — well for a bleak January spent wading through the endless legal documents for the move. Hopes and spirits were high. Then along came the storms.

Storm Brendan wrecked the roof, Ciara claimed the conservatory, Dennis annihilated the chimney and Jorge found his way in through the patio doors.

We set about repairing and renovating, racing against the clock before completion. We also started throwing out our old furniture and appliances — toaster, sofa, dishwasher, dining table, coffee table — they all went.

And just when things were falling into place — contracts signed and sealed, furniture slung, boxes packed — and we were ready to move, along came a global pandemic.

Almost overnight, daily life changed beyond recognition. It was such a terrible time. So many lives lost, so much fear and sadness. I struggled to comprehend what was happening.

I'd been working on a different book for a while (years and years and years) but with all the sadness and anxiety that lockdown brought, I found it impossible to continue. I couldn't concentrate. I struggled with anxiety. The words I needed just wouldn't come. Instead, I wrote about what was happening all around me, locally and nationally, not with any hope of publication, but to capture and try to process what was going on. My words were fragmented and hurried — they didn't make sense, but neither did what was happening in the world.

The more I wrote, the more I tried to find the funny things in life, because being able to laugh, or even just smile, seemed to make the dark days a little brighter. In April, I sat down and wrote 'Living in a germ factory', and then shared it on my blog. It seemed mildly amusing, and I hoped that people might relate to what I was feeling.

Much to my surprise, people read it and said positive things, and some of them even laughed, so I continued writing and sharing these slices of life. It helped me cope with what was happening. And if it made people smile, even better.

This book is a collection of all my life in lockdown stories from 2020. I share the highs and lows of my everyday life during the crazy days of the first peak of the coronavirus crisis, and where I can, try to see the funny side. They are tales of chaos, confusion and cake. Everything in here really happened — some things I wish hadn't (global pandemic obviously, Chris's toe injury, the weight gain). I have grouped the pieces into three sections: 'Life in Lockdown', 'Moving House in a Pandemic' and 'The New Normal'.

They are mostly in chronological order, but you don't have to read them in order — start at the front, in the middle, or even at the back if you wish and dip in and out of them whenever you feel like it. I'd recommend reading with a brew or a slice of cake, or maybe both, because that's what I do when I write — I am fuelled by caffeine and cake. Thanks to writing this book and lockdown life, I'm also a few pounds heavier (actually, it's a stone, but I'm working on it. Now I've finished, I'm going for a run).

Thank you very much for reading my book. I hope you enjoy it, and more than anything, I hope it makes you smile.

Happy reading.

Liz x

P.S. And please get in touch. I'd love to hear from you.

www.lizchampion.co.uk

I

LIFE IN LOCKDOWN

Living in a germ factory

'Do you think you're in news overload?' Chris asks me on Thursday night as we sit down to watch the evening news.

'We have to be informed,' I tell him. 'It's important.'

'But you've got it on all the time. It's not healthy.'

He has a point. After watching the news every hour on the hour for the last six weeks, I've become quite the expert on coronavirus. I know which surfaces it lives on and for how long. I know the symptoms and incubation period. I even know about the complexities of the 'R' rate. I'm so well informed I'm surprised they've not asked me to run Downing Street's daily briefing.

'Shall we have a break from it?' Chris suggests. 'Just for tonight?' He's got a strange, almost desperate look on his face.

I consider telling him to go upstairs and watch what he wants, but he looks like he's about to crumble. Instead, I feel a compromise is in order. 'We'll watch *Channel 4 News* and then something else.'

He breathes a sigh of relief and then disappears into the kitchen to make us a cup of tea while I consume every piece of news available.

I sit on the sofa, staring at the TV, and I can feel my heart rate getting faster, thudding in my chest. It's about this time every night that I develop symptoms. Headache, sore throat, feeling hot — I've had them all, just not at the same time.

'My heart's beating fast,' I tell Chris when he returns with our tea.

'Maybe it's watching so much news.'

'Don't be ridiculous.' I turn back to the TV, steaming mug in hand.

When the hour is up, I've drunk several cups of tea without really noticing, but, thankfully, my heart rate has steadied. 'You're right,' I say. 'We should watch something else, something un-virus related.'

But just as I'm saying this, a trailer comes on for the programme on next — *How Clean is Your House? A coronavirus special*. It promises to explain how coronavirus works, how it uses our behaviour to get into our homes. And what we can do to stop it.

Immediately my heart resumes its frantic thudding. 'We need to watch this,' I say. 'We need to know this stuff.'

The programme follows two families, who seem to have immaculate houses, identifying how and where the virus could infiltrate. The expert provides germ-busting tips and tricks that leave me and the families shaking our heads and looking panicked.

'I've been doing it all wrong,' the woman on TV moans as she mops her floor.

'You're not the only one,' I shout back.

Apparently, we should use a three-mop system. 'We don't even own three mops. Why don't we have three mops?'

They reveal more tips, like sterilising the bleach bottles and sanitising the thermostat.

'I don't do that,' I say after each revelation. 'Do you do that?'

'No,' Chris says. 'I've never even thought about any of it.'

At the end of the programme, my head is swirling. 'We're living in a germ factory.'

Chris looks just as horrified as I feel.

'Don't panic,' I say, grabbing a cloth. 'I'm on it.'

That night, all the next day and into the weekend and bank holiday, I clean. I am not a cleaner. I have never been a cleaner, but I clean and clean and clean.

When Mum rings, I don't have time to chat. 'I'm cleaning,' I say.

'Cleaning?' I hear the shock in her voice.

'Yes. It's taken a global pandemic, but I'm… cleaning.'

'That's good,' she says. 'I'll leave you to it.'

The cleaning continues. There is not an inch of house left untouched. Chris even pops out and buys another mop — essential according to the expert on TV. I feel calm and in control. And then, the last job, the mopping.

Of all the extra cleaning measures, it's the three-mop system that causes the problem. I accidentally mix up the mops, and then use so much bleach, I have to go outside to avert an asthma attack.

While I sit on the patio, breathing in the fresh spring air, Chris stays inside. He runs from window to window, a tea towel over his nose and mouth, letting in air to dilute the toxic fumes.

Suddenly, it all feels too much. I take my newly disinfected phone from my pocket and text my friend. 'I'm having a mopping meltdown.'

Chris steps outside, removing the tea towel from his face.

'I'm sorry,' I tell him. 'I wish we hadn't watched that bloody programme.'

'You were the one who —'

'I know.'

My phone beeps. A reply from my friend. 'I'm here for you in these times of mop-related crises.'

The whiff of bleach has faded when I go back into the house. I put the three mops into the cupboard, put the kettle on, and breathe.

25 April 2020

The world is baking

There is not an ounce of flour to be found anywhere. 'The shelves are empty,' Mum phones to tell me. 'I've looked everywhere.'

'I think I have some,' I say, not wanting to get her hopes up. This is the third time she's mentioned flour — or the lack of it — this week.

'Do you?' She sounds so excited.

'I think so.' In last week's cleaning frenzy, I was sure I'd seen some in a cupboard. 'Let me check.'

Still on the phone, I walk to the kitchen, open the cupboard, and sure enough there is the flour. 'Half a bag,' I tell her.

'That's amazing!'

I look at the opened bag of Be-Ro, which is dusted in flour and torn in places. 'It's seen better days,' I say, taking it out. 'It could have been in here for years.' I try to remember when I last baked a cake, or some buns, or anything, but I can't. 'I'm not sure it's edible.'

'Of course it is. It lasts forever. I can't believe you have flour. That's brilliant.'

'You've not seen it.' I hold it at arm's length.

'Check the best before,' Mum says.

I search the bag for a date. A white sprinkling of flour falls onto my worktops — the ones I've just cleaned. 'I can't find it,' I say, wanting to drop it into the bin before it causes any more mess.

'It'll have a date on it,' Mum says.

And right enough, on the bottom of the bag in faded print, there it is. 'April.' Followed by a year that's too faded to read.

'I'll have to throw it,' I say.

'Oh.' Mum is unable to hide her disappointment.

'Did you want to bake that much?' I ask.

'No, it's fine. We just fancied some cake, really. But we can't use that.'

'I'm sure it'll be back in stock soon.' I try to sound optimistic.

'The entire world is baking,' she grumbles. 'You can't get it anywhere. It's like gold dust. I've more chance of winning the lottery, and I don't even play.'

I hang up, feeling like a disappointing daughter because I don't have a cupboard full of flour.

'We should have stocked up,' I tell Chris. 'It's like the toilet rolls all over again.'

When everyone was bulk-buying loo roll, we'd laughed at their silliness. We soon stopped laughing when we were down to our last roll and couldn't get another anywhere.

I hold the bag of flour up. 'Flour is the new loo roll.'

'Get it on eBay,' Chris says. 'We'll trade it for a penthouse in Chelsea.'

I'm heading to the bin to throw out the flour when I have an idea. 'I'll bake,' I tell him. 'It's only borderline out of date. I'm sure it'll be fine.'

Chris looks at me. 'Are you sure?'

I look again at the best before date — it definitely says April, but I'm not sure if it's 2019 or 2020. I look closer. I consider the current flour crisis. 'I can't throw it away when there's such a shortage. It's not right. I'm going to make Mum and Dad a cake.'

I get to work straightaway. Flour, sugar, margarine, eggs. I consult a James Martin recipe but then do my own thing. I slap on the buttercream and jam, sprinkle some icing sugar on the top. The house smells of home baking. I can't help but feel proud of myself. When things get back to normal, I'll apply to *The Great British Bake Off*, blessed as I am with such a baking talent.

I cut half for us and take the other half to Mum and Dad's, leaving it on the patio table and backing away to a socially acceptable distance.

'Cake!' Mum shouts. 'That's wonderful. Where did you find flour?'

'I had a secret supply,' I say.

She looks at me; she looks at the cake. 'You didn't use that out-of-date flour, did you?'

'No,' I lie. 'I found another bag.'

The next day, Mum phones. 'Your sister's got some flour, so she's baking, too.'

'Is she?' There is no hiding the surprise in my voice.

'She's making Olivia's birthday cake.'

'I would have done it.' My sister, Sarah, has many skills, but I'm not convinced cake-making is one of them.

For the next few days, I worry about the mess she'll make of it. I worry that my soon to be eight-year-old niece will be disappointed.

On the day of the birthday, they reveal the cake over a family video call. Not only has Sarah made a cake, but she's also decorated it creatively using KitKats and M&M's. It puts my slapped-on jam and buttercream to shame.

'Look at that,' Chris says. 'You've been outdone.'

'Have you made that?' I ask.

'It was a team effort.' She nods to her partner, who smiles smugly at his cake-making capabilities.

We sing happy birthday and watch them eat the cake.

'Mmm,' they say. 'Delicious.'

I hang up, head for the kitchen and cut the last few slices of my cake.

Chris takes a bite.

11

I hear it crunch, not a good sign for a supposedly soft and fluffy sponge.

'It does have a strange taste,' he says.

'It's the flour,' I say. 'I think it went out of date in 2018.'

2 May 2020

Piling on the pounds

My shorts have shrunk. I stand in front of the mirror, trying to fasten the denim cut-offs that fitted perfectly last summer.

I stretch and pull the material and somehow manage to force the button and hole together. For a second, I feel victorious but then realise that all the fat around my waist has been pushed upwards. I now have a muffin top.

'Chris! Look what's happened.'

He comes running upstairs. 'What's wrong?' he says.

'Either the shorts have shrunk, or I've got fatter.'

He looks at them, tilting his head to one side. 'Are they the ones you wore on holiday last year?'

'Yes!'

'They didn't look like that then.'

'I know!'

Last year, we'd celebrated my fortieth birthday on a former leper colony in Crete (if you've read Victoria Hislop's *The Island*, you'll understand). But the only way I could cope with becoming so old was by making sure I looked good on the day. It had taken quite a bit of work. In the months and weeks leading up to it, I'd embarked on a healthy eating and fitness regime that had required willpower of steel. I'd lost a stone, felt amazing and been so proud of myself.

Seven weeks into lockdown, and I realise that most of the hard work has been undone.

I turn to look at the shorts from behind. They don't look good. Fat from the top of my legs and bum has been pushed down and is now bulging out below the shorts in two rolls.

'Do you think it's because I've been doing some strength training?' I ask, thinking about the workout with Joe Wicks last week.

Chris laughs. 'No. I think it's because you've been doing reps to the fridge.'

I say nothing. I look at my barely there shorts and bigger body. Life during lockdown has involved less exercise and more eating. But I am not alone in the fridge reps; my fridge reps are his fridge reps.

'Do you feel fat?' I ask.

'I feel chubby.' He pats his stomach. 'We'll have to cut out the chocolate.'

'That's a bit drastic.' I think about our chocolate stash.

While everyone was out bulk buying loo rolls, I'd cleared the neighbourhood of Dairy Milk, Minstrels and Maltesers. They'd been hard to get hold of. I'd had to raid the local corner shop.

'People have gone mad,' I'd told the shop owner, grabbing bag after bag. 'Absolutely crackers.'

'Is that everything?' she'd asked. 'I have some of those enormous bars of Galaxy you like.'

'I'll take them all,' I'd said.

We now have enough chocolate to last the year, if not the decade.

'We can't waste it,' I tell Chris. 'We'll have to take the fitness approach to weight loss instead.'

In the first few weeks of lockdown, I was very focused,

running 5k a day and joining in with Joe. But by week four, I'd abandoned them in favour of writing. I've been at my keyboard frantically typing most days since. The only problem is that writing involves several hundred cups of tea and a bar or two of chocolate. Only two, though. I have limits.

But in lockdown, there has been no limit to my snacking. In a world of uncertainty, the fridge runs are my only constant.

'We need to take action,' I say. 'Before it gets out of hand.'

So, on Monday morning, I reintroduce my morning 5k run. Then, in my Zoom meeting with work colleagues, I suggest I write a feature about how to stop snacking.

'I'm sure other people must be struggling,' I tell my colleagues. 'It can't just be me.'

'It's not,' my boss says. 'I'll need a crane to get me out of the house if I carry on.'

'I've been terrible,' I say. 'I've started having brunch (toast with full-fat butter and jam) as well as breakfast and have introduced a cereal course into the afternoon to get me through the daily briefing. Then there's the biscuits while I'm working.'

'A cereal course?' She shakes her head. 'You've taken it to a whole new level.'

'Don't make me feel bad,' I say. 'It's like I'm trapped on the world's worst all-inclusive.'

That afternoon, I make a cup of tea and settle down to write. I know nothing about how to stop snacking, so I start with some research. I find some ideas, like drink lots of water, plan your meals and chew slowly.

'Do you want a biscuit?' Chris asks.

'No!'

'Are you sure?'

'Are you having one?'

16

'Yes.'

'What are you having?'

'Maltesers biscuits.'

The Maltesers biscuits are a recent discovery after an online-shop substitution. We'd ordered flour and got biscuits. I think about the honeycomb and smooth chocolate, all deliciously put together in a biscuit.

'I'll just have one.'

Chris holds out the packet. I take one and they call to me. I take another and return to my research.

The psychology of eating is fascinating stuff.

'I've been emotional eating.' I take a bite of the biscuit and read out my findings. 'Emotional eating is when you're bored, stressed, anxious, unhappy or sad, and you eat for that reason, not because you're actually hungry.'

Chris listens.

'It all makes sense,' I say. 'It's an emotional time.'

My chocolate binges have mainly happened when I've been watching the news and I'm hit by emotion overload — sadness, anxiety, unhappiness, more sadness, more anxiety, more un-happiness. Before even thinking about what I'm doing, I've run to the fridge, grabbed a family bar of Dairy Milk and scoffed the lot.

I read on. 'Recognising when you do this is the first step in taking action to control it.' I take another bite of the biscuit, then start on biscuit number two. I am pleased that I can now recognise emotional eating and, when the time arises, put strategies in place to stop the snacking.

I walk to the fridge, take a third biscuit. They really are delicious. I chew slowly, enjoying its crunchiness. It really is the little things.

'Going without chocolate would be very stressful.'

Chris nods. 'We don't need more stress.'

The next day the sun is shining. I take my shorts from the wardrobe and crowbar myself into them.

'I'm embracing my curves,' I say. 'Dieting's for another day.'

9 May 2020

Dad's socially distanced 70th

Dad is turning 70 during lockdown. We cancel the surprise family holiday to Craster.

Here's what you could have won, I write in his card, including a picture of the beautiful Northumberland coast.

Then I go online and order a badge saying '70 effing hell'; a T-shirt with 'born in 1950 — original parts mostly' printed on it; and a book about dad cars of bygone years. There's also a card with Boris Johnson on the front, saying 'Don't forget to wash your hands.'

'It's not much really,' I say when everything arrives.

'He'll just be pleased that the country's in lockdown so you can't spring a surprise party on him,' Chris says.

'I know. But he can't turn 70 with no fuss. We'll have to do something.'

I phone my sister. 'Any ideas for Dad's birthday? Legal, without breaking government guidelines.'

'I was thinking homemade afternoon tea,' she says. 'We can make it and drop it off.'

'That sounds good. I'd kill for afternoon tea.'

'I'll make the sandwiches, quiche and scones,' she says. 'You make the cake.'

We form a plan: her on savoury, me on sweet.

'That's a winning combination,' Chris says. 'You and your sister in charge of catering.'

'It'll be fine,' I say. 'I'm sure we can rustle up some sandwiches and cake between us.'

The day before the birthday, I get to work on the cake. I double the ingredients of a normal-sized Victoria sandwich. 'It's going to be special,' I say. 'Think *Bake Off* showstopper.'

When I take it out of the oven, it looks impressive, bigger than any cake I have ever made.

There's always a worry it'll get stuck in the tin, but one quick flip and it's out.

'Perfect.' I imagine Paul Hollywood admiring my scrumptious sponge. It's bound to be a winner.

While it's cooling, I make a batch of basic buns. 'Who knew I was such a domestic goddess?'

Everything is fine until I try to transfer the cake from the cooling rack onto a plate ready for the all-important decorating. I lift, but it won't budge. I pull harder. Part of the cake comes off; the other half stays firmly welded to the rack. And then the middle drops out.

'Chris! Look what's happened!'

Chris comes running in, that familiar look of panic on his face. Between us, we extricate the sponge from the rack and shove it back into the centre of the cake.

'A bit of jam and buttercream and you'll not be able to tell,' he says.

I slap on the jam and buttercream — a bit here, a bit there. And then comes the tricky bit: putting the two parts of the cake together. I take a deep breath and quickly drop one on top of the other. For a second it looks perfect, but slowly, the weight of the top layer presses down and jam seeps down the sides.

'And it's leaning,' Chris says.

I straighten it up, but more jam oozes out. 'It's a disaster.'

'Rustic. Your dad will love it.'

I look at the leaning mess of a cake. 'He will, but my sister won't. She's got standards.' I think of her scrutinising stare. 'She'll have something to say about it.'

There's nothing else for it. On the morning of Dad's birthday, I start again. This time, I abandon my grand plans in favour of a much smaller bake. I spread the jam thinly, add the buttercream, sprinkle some icing sugar on top. 'Ta-dah!' I proudly show off version two. 'She couldn't possibly say anything about this one.'

'What flavour jam did you use?' Chris asks.

'Strawberry.'

'Isn't she allergic to strawberries?'

I look from Chris to the cake, then back to Chris. 'Shit.'

'One mouthful and that'll kill her.'

'She'll have to eat the buns instead. I can't go through the ordeal of making another.'

We load up the car with cake and buns, put the dogs in the back, and drive to Mum and Dad's. On the way, we stop off at a friend's and leave the first cake on her doorstep. It's so heavy I can feel my biceps burning.

'Is this an essential trip?' Chris asks.

'Yes! Cake is essential.'

We arrive at my parents' house at the same time as Sarah and her partner. She's carrying a tray of sandwiches (homemade), Yorkshire Tea, and quiche, scones and pork pies still in their packaging.

'Didn't you make them?' I'm unsure what part of homemade afternoon tea she doesn't understand.

'No!' She looks at me like I've just suggested the unthinkable. 'I'm not Nigella.'

I hold up my cake and smile. 'I made this. But I used strawberry jam.'

'I thought you'd forget my allergy.' She raises her eyebrows. 'Actually, a traditional Victoria sandwich is made with raspberry jam.'

'Nothing traditional about this one,' I say, marching round to Mum and Dad's back door.

We take our socially distanced places on opposite ends of the patio. Mum and Dad are in the middle but indoors, peering out of the open door.

'Surprise,' I shout, revealing the cake.

'Surprise,' Sarah shouts, holding up the tray.

'Not today,' Dad says. 'We're in lockdown.'

Mum elbows him out of the way. 'You've made afternoon tea!' She's unable to hide the excitement in her voice. 'Who'd have thought it? And Liz is cleaning now, too. She's even disinfecting her door handles.'

Of all the things I've done in my life, it's the door handles that seem to instil the most pride.

She turns to Sarah. 'And have you put on any weight? Liz has.'

'It depends which tile I put the scales on,' Sarah says. 'I'm the thinnest I've ever been, or not...'

'Hold the wall,' I tell her. 'It takes pounds off.'

We spend the rest of the afternoon standing in the freezing cold, chatting and eating. It's like the family is together again, just not actually within touching distance. The only thing missing is my niece, who is at her dad's for the weekend. So we sit and talk about the funny things she says and does.

I don't want the day to end but the temperature has plummeted, frostbite is setting in and the dogs need walking before we head home.

We wave goodbye and set off on our walk. I feel happy that we've seen them, but sad that we can't do the things we usually do — like sit in the kitchen with the central heating on.

We're a mile into the walk when a car comes towards us with a child hanging out of the window, shouting and waving.

'Someone needs to get that child under control,' I say before realising that the child in question belongs to us.

'Auntie Liz. I'm doing a drive-by for Granddad's birthday.'

I stand at the side of the road, trying to hold back my tears. 'I've not seen you for eight weeks. Love you.'

She gives another wave.

'What a lovely end to a lovely day,' Chris says as we watch the car disappear into the distance.

'Perfect,' I say, letting the tears fall.

16 May 2020

Is it stress?

I stand in front of the mirror feeling dizzy and a little sick. At first, I thought it was the light catching on my hair and making it shine. I even thought it was my natural blonde starting to come through after weeks of lockdown. But, on closer inspection, I realise I am wrong.

'Chris,' I say. 'Look at this.'

He comes into the room. 'When did that happen?'

Before the virus, there'd been one or two strands, hardly worth bothering about. But there's no ignoring the recent ones. They sprout from my head, demanding to be noticed. Almost overnight, it's like they've taken over my scalp.

I stare into the mirror and an older version of me looks back.

'It's the stress. It has to be the stress!'

I grab my phone and do what I always do in times of emergency.

'Dad, it's me.'

'She's not in,' he says.

'Not in?'

'No. She's gone to the garden centre. She'll be back in September.'

'That's not essential. What's she doing?'

'Bedding plants,' Dad says, as though that explains everything.

'It'll take more than a global pandemic to stop your mother from getting her geraniums.'

I hang up and take another look at my hair. My heart is beating quickly, the panic overwhelming. Desperate times call for desperate measures, so I call my sister.

'I'm going grey,' I shout.

'What?'

'My hair!'

She doesn't say anything.

'Every new bit of hair coming through is grey. It's the stress.'

'You're going grey because you're forty-one,' she says.

'I'm not forty-one! I'm forty-and-three-quarters and it is the stress!'

'Well calm down. Or you'll end up completely grey.'

'How do I stop it? Can I stop it?'

'I don't know,' she says. 'I've got enough to worry about with my own roots. Although they are not grey. Definitely not.'

I get off the phone and consult Google. Can stress cause grey hair?

Yes. Stress is terrible for the body. Stress has the power to strip your full head of colour, not to mention causing strokes and heart attacks. Stress is a nasty, evil thing.

I take a deep breath. 'I need to de-stress,' I tell Chris.

He's sitting at the dining room table, staring at a spreadsheet. He looks as stressed as I feel. 'Can you do it upstairs? I've got a call.'

I go back to Google to find out the best ways to de-stress. 'I'll do some yoga,' I say, but he's not listening.

I set up my yoga studio on the landing, with the dogs watching from the top step. I find an online video, a twenty-six-minute stress melt — perfect, it says, for these challenging times.

Why it's precisely twenty-six minutes, I do not understand. Perhaps there's some scientific evidence showing that twenty-six minutes is the ideal time to melt away the stress and strains of lockdown life. Maybe it should get a mention on the briefing.

The yoga class is led by an American woman.

'Well done, y'all,' she says. 'That's sweet. You're doing sweet.'

Everything is sweet. I can feel my blood pressure rising every time she says it. I try to focus on the movements and not the number of 'sweets'.

I'm in down dog position when one of my dogs comes closer, trying to sniff my face. 'Get away,' I tell him. He moves in front of the screen, fascinated by yoga woman.

'Let your mind go.' Her voice is calm and soothing. 'Focus on your breathing.'

I breathe in and out.

'Disconnect your mind from your body. And let your mind's eye fly to a place of peace and tranquillity. Wherever you want to go.' She takes a deep breath. 'In a world of uncertainty, you can choose how to respond. You can choose to be calm.'

I lie on the carpet, with the dogs inching ever closer, and just as I'm severing mind from body (and in my mind boarding a plane to Greece) my phone rings. I jump up, my heart rate soaring.

'I'm back,' Mum says. 'Did you want me?'

It takes a few seconds for my body and mind to reconnect. For those few seconds, it's like everything is fine in the world. And then it all comes back to me. I can feel the colour draining from my hair.

'Are you there?' Mum says. 'I've been to the garden centre. I've got some plants for you.'

'What are you doing risking your life at the garden centre?'

'Alan Titchmarsh says it's an excellent idea. Being in the garden is good for the body, the mind, everything.'

'Mum, you're seventy. You're at risk.'

'I'm not seventy for a few months.'

'Yes, but Mum, you need to be careful.'

'Oh, Elizabeth!' She only calls me that when she's cross. 'I've had a lovely afternoon with the bedding plants.'

'I'm worried,' I say. 'My hair's going grey.'

'You're worrying too much.' She sighs. 'I'll go grey worrying about you worrying too much.'

'Why aren't you grey already?' She's thirty years older than me and only has one or two strands.

'I think you take after Dad. He went grey around the time you were born… You need to calm down.'

'I'm trying. I'm in the middle of yoga.'

'Good. I'll leave you to it. You should think about doing some gardening. The bedding plants look lovely. All that colour and life. It's wonderful.'

I hang up and return to the yoga. Just as I'm trying to float off to a Greek island, there's a knock at the door. The dogs start barking.

'It's a delivery,' Chris shouts. 'I'll get it.'

The barking is too much. I peel myself from the floor and go downstairs. 'Shall we sit out for five minutes?' I say.

I make us both a cup of tea and we sit on the patio in the sunshine, listening to next door's water feature. I've never made time for sitting in the garden and relaxing. I can see why Mum loves it. It does feel like the stress is melting away.

I close my eyes. I relax.

And then there's a knock at the gate. Mum peers over the top. 'Only me,' she says. 'I've got your plants.'

I run my fingers through my greying hair. I think about yoga woman's words of wisdom. 'In a world of uncertainty, you can choose how to respond. You can be calm.'

I take a deep breath, then I go into the shed, pick up a trowel and start digging.

23 May 2020

We need a wedding

'It's our wedding anniversary,' Mum phones to tell me. 'We have cake. Are you calling?'

'Of course. I'll never turn down cake.'

'That's good,' Mum says. 'Your sister's coming too, but don't let that put you off.'

'Right.' There is a brief silence, both of us contemplating the force that is my sister. 'What kind of cake?'

'You'll see.'

'Why are you being secretive?'

'I'm not,' she says, hanging up.

I walk into the kitchen where Chris is staring at a spreadsheet. 'It's their wedding anniversary. Mum sounded a bit... odd.'

'Maybe it's all those years married to your dad,' he says, not looking up.

'She's up to something,' I say. 'She'll be out shopping or something else just as dangerous. I know her.'

I spend the rest of the day working from home wondering what my mother is up to. It's a long day — trying to finish everything before I take a week off for our should-have-been-going-away-but-aren't holiday. Then we drive to Mum and Dad's for a socially distanced patio gathering.

As usual, we're the last to arrive. Mum and Dad are at the

end of the garden, on a table for two. My sister and her partner are on the patio, on the cushioned chairs.

'We don't have any emergency chairs,' Dad says. 'So, it's the bench or the wall.'

'Looks like we're in the cheap seats,' I say to Chris, perching on the wall.

'Nothing new there,' he says, joining me.

'Do you want cake?' Mum's already on her feet, heading towards the kitchen, a big smile on her face.

'You should call more often,' I say to my sister. 'There's always cake when you visit.'

'It's because she lives far away,' Mum shouts through the kitchen window. 'Not because she's the favourite.'

I don't mention that sixteen miles isn't that far.

She returns carrying a tray of food. 'We have chocolate and cream cupcakes, jam tarts, apple pie and Victoria sponge.' She parades up and down the patio — proudly showing off the food while keeping her distance.

It's not the homemade slapped together cake I'd been expecting. This is in packaging, which means a shop has taken place.

'Where did you get all that?' I ask.

'Don't be cross. I went to the farm shop.'

'Mum! Why? You're supposed to be staying in. You can't be risking your life for a jam tart.'

'They're good jam tarts,' Dad says.

'That's why you were being so secretive.' I look to my sister for back up. 'She's going out too much.'

'You need to stay in,' my sister says using her work voice of authority, the one that makes us all tremble in fear.

Mum looks startled but nods, like a chastised child.

'I've done an online shop for them today,' I say, thinking this is the ideal time to get my sister on side and finally end Mum's gallivanting. 'There's no point having online deliveries if she's going here, there and everywhere. In the space of a week, she's been to the garden centre, dentist, doctor's and now the farm shop!'

A look of horror flashes across my sister's face. She fixes her eyes on Mum. 'Well, stay away from me. You could be riddled with disease.'

'I'm not sure the online shop is working out,' Mum says. 'We don't need 480 tea bags.'

'I got the sizes wrong,' I say. I'd been as shocked as her when the sack load of tea arrived. 'We'll have some. We'll get through them in a week.'

'There's a giant-sized butter, too,' Dad says, holding his hands apart to show just how big. 'Massive.'

'All right! I'll take more notice of the sizes,' I say.

'Can we change the subject?' Mum says. 'Eat cake.'

I take a cupcake and a jam tart. 'It's years since I've eaten a jam tart.' It's delicious — sticky and sweet, perfectly proportioned with crumbly pastry. I'm secretly pleased about the farm shop bakes.

'So, what's new?' Mum says.

'Nothing,' I say.

'Nothing,' my sister says.

'I bought a lawn mower,' Dad says. 'And before you ask, it's essential to me.'

I finish the jam tart, move on to the cake.

'It's our anniversary,' Mum reminds us. 'Forty-seven years.'

Almost half a century, I think. 'That's a long time.'

She turns to Dad. 'We had a lovely day. I'm not sure if the guests did. Your dad left your mother the day after, so they can't have enjoyed it that much... But we had a lovely time.'

'It was windy,' Dad says.

'We need another wedding.' I look directly at my sister's partner, who has been sitting quietly eating his Victoria sponge. 'I need something to be thin for.'

He smiles, looks down at his cake.

'It's a shame you weren't at our wedding,' I say to him, keen to continue the wedding chat. Three years ago, she hadn't met him. She'd brought her old flame — the one we didn't like — and then dumped him a few months afterwards.

On the day, I had a feeling the guy would be getting the red card soon. I'd wanted to ask him to step aside so we could have a family photo without him, but I didn't want to be rude. When the album arrived, he was on every shot.

I'd had no choice but to Photoshop him out, replacing his head with sky, and his body with grass. Now all that's left is a little shadow where his head used to be.

I don't mention any of this to my sister's new chap as he sits there eating his sponge.

'There's nothing like a wedding,' I tell him instead. 'And we need something to look forward to.'

'Lovely cake,' he says.

'I could be a bridesmaid again.' Just thinking about it sparks a flicker of not quite excitement, but hope. A wedding will lift all our spirits.

I look to Mum to see if she agrees, but she's shaking her head.

'You're not subtle,' she says.

In my mind, it's perfectly clear. 'When all this is over, we definitely need a wedding.'

I'm just about to ask my brother-in-law-to-be when he's

thinking of proposing, but he's on his feet, practically running down the drive, my sister right behind him.

'What did I say?'

'The poor man is just coming to terms with living with her,' Dad says. 'And now you've terrified him.'

I take another jam tart and watch the happy couple drive into the distance. 'He'll change his mind,' I say. 'Shall we have a sweepstake on when he'll propose.'

31 May 2020

II

MOVING HOUSE IN A PANDEMIC

For sale

The estate agent calls at five o'clock on Friday evening, just as we're talking about his lack of interest in our house.

'You've got a viewer,' he says in a very excited voice. 'Sunday morning at eleven.'

'That's great.' I try to match his excitement. 'Thank you.' I hang up and turn to Chris. 'We've got a viewer.'

'That's brilliant!' Chris looks relieved more than excited. 'I didn't think anyone was interested.'

'I'm not sure they are,' I say. 'He must have known we were complaining, so found us someone from somewhere.'

'He can't just conjure up a viewer.'

'I'll bet he can.'

Chris sighs. 'Fake viewers. He's probably got them on standby... But at least someone's coming, so that's good.'

I look around at the house. 'We'll have to tidy up.' Since we stuffed everything in drawers and cupboards, on a mission to make the house appear minimalist for the marketing photos, things have started to creep back. Every surface is cluttered with books and papers and things. 'I wouldn't want to buy it, looking like this. Would you?'

Chris shakes his head. 'Definitely not.'

We begin the de-cluttering process immediately, putting things back into cupboards and drawers, forcing in as much as we can. 'I hope they don't open anything,' Chris says. 'It'll all fall out.'

'It's the house they're buying, not the drawers.'

We work late into the night, throwing some things away, saving others. I see the overwhelm creeping into Chris's face.

'You've got a lot of stuff.' He stands in the middle of the room, looking lost. 'And books.' He shakes his head. 'You've got so many.'

Not the books again. Chris is sounding like my dad, who has been trying to persuade me to throw all my books away since the beginning of time. 'I'll get a skip,' he always says. 'And you can chuck the lot.'

The thought of throwing out books makes me feel sick. So I never do. And my book collection just keeps growing and growing. Years ago, at university, my tutor would encourage us to buy books. 'It's another one for the shelf,' he'd say.

The shelf became two shelves and then three and four. Then a bookcase, and another and another, and then a room. Now they're spilling over into every corner and on every bit of surface available, stacked on the floor, on the desk, on top of bookcases, and piled on the carpet.

'I like books,' I say.

'But they've taken over.'

'That's why we need a bigger house.'

'But no one is going to buy this one because of the books.'

'We might get someone who enjoys reading.'

He points towards the book room. 'They can't even get in there.'

'They can.'

'They can't. I've not been in that room for years.'

'Well, I have.'

'Only if you crowbar yourself in.'

He has a point. For years, we've had to open the door and squeeze in sideways. The library is packed into a six-foot box room, with books stacked floor to ceiling. Chris hasn't dared go inside in case one of the book towers comes crashing down.

'What are we going to do with it?' He shakes his head again. 'What was it the estate agent said when he took the photos? Not to show the book room in the brochure because it's our Achilles heel.'

'He's obviously not much of a reader… And can we get on with it?'

It is late. I am tired. But we work into the night. Chris sorts the rest of the house, while I focus on transforming the book room into something resembling an organised library.

'Look,' I open the door and step in. 'They can get in now.'

Chris smiles. 'It's coming together.'

By the time we go to bed, the house is looking less like a hovel and more like a show home. Although show home is probably taking it too far.

That night I dream about my new library. It has an armchair in the corner, and there's floor-to-ceiling bookcases, with a ladder to reach the top shelves, and it's huge.

When I wake up, I am happy, revived almost, keen to make the dream a reality. Doubts about never finding such a place, and fears of not being able to afford it even if we did, creep into my mind. I push them away and try to stay positive.

With the decluttering finished, the big clean up begins early on
Saturday morning. Out come the hoover and cleaning products,
my asthmatic lungs tightening at the sight of them.

Mum phones when I'm halfway through disinfecting the
bathroom. 'Do you fancy a shopping trip?'

'Me?' I say, thinking she's phoned the wrong daughter.

'Yes, I don't mind waiting while you go in the bookshop.'

'Really?' Usually, she's the one dragging me out.

'Your sister's busy. And we've not had a day out together for
ages.'

'We're sorting the house,' I say. 'We've got a viewer coming in
the morning.'

'Have you?' Mum's voice inches higher. 'We'll come and help.
I love an interiors project.'

Within ten minutes, she and Dad have arrived and are rolling up their sleeves ready to get stuck into some work. Mum's attention is inside, Dad's out.

'I've brought my pressure washer,' he says. 'I'll give the conservatory roof a good blast.'

'Do you know what you're doing, Dad?'

'Do I know what I'm doing?' He shakes his head in that of-course-I-know-what-I'm-doing-I'm-your-dad way.

'With all the rain, there's a layer of green slime on it,' I tell him.

'No problem. I'll get that off.' He nods and heads outside.

'Be careful,' Mum shouts after him. 'There's a storm coming.' Outside the wind is whipping up, the trees blowing wildly.

Dad is already outside, ladders propped against the house, putting his first foot on the rung. A feeling of dread stirs in the pit of my stomach, as I watch my soon to be seventy-year-old dad climb onto the conservatory.

'There's no stopping him,' Mum says. 'His dad was the same. I remember him falling through the loft when I was staying over once.' She laughs at the memory. 'He came straight through the ceiling.'

I stare up at Dad. 'I hope that doesn't happen. We'd never sell the house.'

We work for hours, stopping briefly to refuel with cups of tea and sandwiches before resuming work. By the end of the day, the house is transformed.

'It looks amazing.' Mum gives her verdict. 'I have a good feeling about this viewer.'

And with their work done, they go on their way.

The storm comes overnight. Yorkshire is already underwater from storm Brendan, so Ciara makes a bad situation worse. She rattles the windows and keeps us awake, disrupting my library dreams.

When I wake up the next morning, I'm relieved that there's no more work to do. The house is immaculate. I stay in bed, knowing I can have a leisurely start to the day. I read for a while, before going downstairs to make a brew.

I hear the water before I see it — not a light trickle, more a ferocious gushing. Rain is sliding down the wall and running along the ceiling to the light-fitting where a spectacular waterfall cascades onto the table.

'Chris!' I grab a pan and put it under the leak. 'Chris!'

'What's happened?' He comes rushing into the room, sees the water and freezes. 'What the…?'

Water crashes through the ceiling. I stand underneath the deluge in my dressing gown, optimistically holding up the pan to catch it. 'What shall we do?'

Within a second, he's regained his composure. 'Turn off the light. And the electric in case the entire house goes up in flames.'

I do as he says. That really would shatter our moving plans.

He grabs some towels and a mop and bucket and runs around the kitchen frantically trying to stop the flow.

'What are we going to do?' I wail. 'The viewers are coming at eleven.'

'We'll have to cancel.'

I grab my phone and call the estate agent. It goes straight to answerphone.

'Our offices open at eleven,' the cheery voice recording says.

I hang up. 'They're shut until eleven! The viewers will be here then.' Panic is rising almost as fast as the tide in the kitchen.

'Your dad must have done something when he cleaned the roof.'

45

I think of Dad with his pressure washer. He's used so much pressure he's blasted a layer off the kitchen roof.

I pick up a towel and join Chris in his drying-out efforts. 'What are we going to say when they knock on the door?'

Chris stops what he's doing and stares out of the window. 'The rain's easing, so hopefully this might have stopped by then.'

'It won't! And there's still all these water marks everywhere!'

'Let's just calm down,' he says, looking anything but calm.

I take a deep breath and burst out laughing. 'Can you believe this is happening?'

'Not really.'

'It's ridiculous. We've viewed some absolute hovels, but not one of them has had water pouring through the roof. If they had, I would have walked straight out. That's what these viewers will do.'

Chris nods. The look on his face makes me want to wrap my arms around him. Moving house is turning into quite an ordeal.

'Don't worry.' For Chris's sake, I try to sound positive. 'I'm going to sell it. I'll market it as a water feature.'

A few minutes before eleven, the water is still dripping, splashing into the pan with force. The sound reverberates around the house. I place a tea towel over the top, muffling the sound.

'Be positive and smiley,' I tell Chris when they arrive. He forces a half-smile, the least smiley person in the world.

I open the door, smile widely. 'We've had a slight problem.' And I flash another huge grin.

Half an hour later, I'm smiling so much my face is hurting. We've shown them around, answered their questions and done our best to sell the house, although most of it is now underwater.

The minute they pull off the drive, my smile fades. 'I'm glad that ordeal's over. I was as false as that estate agent.'

'We were honest,' Chris says, as though they should commend us.

'What else could we do with a tsunami in the kitchen?'

The phone rings. It's Dad.

'Liz! I've been worrying. You know that moss I took off yesterday?'

'Yes?'

'I think it was holding the roof together. The roof wasn't in a good way. I nearly put my foot through it. And with all the rain last night... Is it okay?'

'It's been better.'

Mum and Dad come round to investigate the mess he's made, and we call in the professionals. Just as the flood is receding, and the roofers are getting to work, and I'm sitting down with my first brew of the day, the estate agent calls.

'They like the house.'

'Really?'

'Yes, they'd like a second viewing. Without the waterfall, obviously. And they'd like to make an offer.'

'Blimey...' I arrange a day and time for them to return, and hang up. I turn to my family who gather around me, anxiously awaiting an update.

'They liked it,' I say.

'They weren't fake viewers?' Chris says.

'No.' I shake my head. 'But how could anyone like it when the roof's about to cave in?'

'They could obviously see past that,' Mum says. 'It's a nice house.'

Dad exhales loudly. 'I thought I'd ruined your chances.'

I look at the ceiling. The water has slowed to a trickle.

Mum claps her hands together. 'I told you, I had a good feeling about them.'

8 February 2020

On the move

I wake at 4.30am, grab my phone and do what I do every morning — search for an online shop. Most slots between now and Christmas are taken, but I keep scrolling and just as I'm about to give up, one becomes available.

'I've got one!' I say to Chris, who is still sleeping. 'I'm winning at life!'

He grunts and turns over, pulling the sheets further over his head.

Shop secured, I go downstairs, make a cup of tea, and assess the chaos that has become our living room. There are boxes and books everywhere.

I have three and a half hours to sort it all before the removal team arrives. I finish my tea and set to work. I move quickly, packing the books and stacking the boxes.

My aim is to be as organised as possible, which is difficult because it's not in my nature. And given that the move is today, it's a bit last minute.

At six o'clock I realise that Chris isn't up. 'Chris,' I shout. 'Get up!'

'It's only six o'clock,' he shouts back, his voice heavy with sleep.

'I know! And you should be up. We're moving!'

Packing done, I start dismantling the furniture. Then I open every window in the house.

'Why is it so cold?' Chris asks when he finally gets up.

'I'm creating the outdoors indoors,' I tell him. 'So, there's less chance of catching the virus.'

'I'll take the dogs for a walk,' he says. 'It'll be warmer.'

'It's half-past six,' I tell him.

While he's out, I put a mattress cover on each mattress, take the final meter readings, and start cleaning.

Chris and the dogs return from their walk, slightly more awake than when they left, but not by much.

'You need to move quicker,' I tell him.

'I need to go for petrol,' he says.

'Petrol?'

He nods.

'Why didn't you get petrol last night? There's no time for petrol! I have a million jobs for you.'

'I don't want to risk running out,' he says, heading for the door.

'It's almost seven!' I shout after him.

While he drives to the petrol station, I continue my house-move mission. Since getting the keys to our new house a week ago, I've been a one-woman removal team, moving boxes (mainly books) from the old house to the new house in my tiny car. I've done about a thousand trips. Chris, meanwhile, struggled to get the time off work. He's been sitting in the old house staring at a spreadsheet.

'Why not leave it all to the removal firm?' he suggests.

'I want them in and out,' I tell him. 'Touching as little as possible.'

So, I continue on my own. I move the books. I call the

gas and electricity and water people. I master not one but two council tax online forms. I empty the loft, discovering what I think is a body, but is actually a Christmas tree with a receipt showing that the previous house owners purchased it from Woolworths in 1995 for £14.95. I order a skip. I fill the skip. I speak to solicitors and the housebuilder, then talk to the removal team about PPE and how we can all stay safe. I stock up on antibacterial wipes and hand sanitiser and then order face masks.

I get up when the sun rises and don't stop until after it has set. This is a move of military precision and it's coming together.

'What needs doing?' Chris asks when he returns from getting petrol.

'Nothing. I've done everything.'

He looks at me as though he can't quite believe it.

'Everything,' I say again. 'There is not one job that I haven't thought of and done.'

'You've done well,' he says. 'Amazingly well. You've not stopped.'

'I know. I'm like Superwoman!'

Feeling organised for the first time in my life, I put the kettle on. It is 7.45am.

As I sip my tea and assess the organised scene before me, a seed of doubt works its way into my mind. 'I've forgotten something,' I say.

'You haven't.'

'I have. There's definitely something... I don't know what.'

It's not until two hours later, when the removal team are mid-way through emptying the old house, that I remember. 'I haven't fed the horses!'

When I arrive, they are standing at the gate stamping their

feet and snorting. 'Sorry,' I shout, jumping out of the car. 'I am so, so sorry.'

The nice pony nudges me with his head, but not in the gentle, affectionate way he usually does. This is so forceful I almost topple over. The nasty pony nips my backside. The horse can't control herself and rears up in rage.

'I'm sorry,' I say again.

They barge me out of the way and make the charge for breakfast. I stand and watch them eat, feeling like a failure.

Getting up and feeding the horses has been part of my routine since I was twelve. I would drag myself out of bed and sort them before school. During my teens and early twenties (my clubbing years), I'd turn them out on my way home in the early hours. They have always been my priority. Until now. In the midst of a global pandemic, they are taking second place to the online shop.

'You're late,' Mum says, heading out on her morning walk. 'I could hear them whinnying from inside the house.'

'Why didn't you call me?'

'I've never had to remind you.'

'I forgot them! I'm such a bad mother.'

Mum stops and stares at me. 'You've a lot on your mind. Moving house is one of the most stressful things you can do, almost as bad as divorce.'

'That's coming next,' I say. 'Once I've recovered from this ordeal.'

'Don't take it out on Chris.' She walks on, leaving me standing in the field.

With the horses now calm and eating, I feel better. I should get back to the chaos of the move, but I can't face it yet. I stand and breathe, enjoying the fresh air, and, apart from the munching of hungry horses, the silence.

The pheasant that has taken up residency in the bushes at the bottom of the field struts around, pecking the ground. He too looks hungry, preoccupied with the hunt for food. He's so preoccupied that he doesn't sense the danger coming his way.

I see it first — a shadow in the undergrowth, a cat, low on the ground, ready to pounce.

Then he spots it, lets out a panicked squawk and starts running and flapping for his life. The cat makes its move and so do I, running and waving and shouting, making it go elsewhere for breakfast.

When the coast is clear, the bird ventures back out. He looks at me. I look at him.

'Thank you,' he seems to say. 'You saved me.'

'It's a good job I was late,' I tell him.

I lock the gate and walk away, happy that my Superwoman status has been restored.

21 June 2020

The right and wrong way to put up a bed

It's the first night in our new home and something doesn't feel right. I sit in bed, eyes scanning the room, trying to work out exactly what.

'Something's not right,' I say to Chris.

'I know what you mean.' He is lying next to me also scanning the room.

Our furniture has been taken down in the old house and put up in the new house. Things seem the same but aren't.

'It feels... wrong,' I say. 'The wardrobe looks massive. It didn't look like that before.'

'No.' He looks the wardrobe up and down. 'It looks huge.'

'Either we're really low down or the wardrobe has grown,' I say.

'We'll get used to it,' he says.

'We won't. It has to be right.'

'Tomorrow. We'll sort it tomorrow.' He closes his eyes and within seconds is sleeping.

I fall asleep, but the wardrobe is on my mind, drifting into my dreams. It looms above me, taking on a strange and sinister shape. In the morning, everything still feels wrong.

'We're too low down.' I wake Chris. 'I feel like we're on the floor.'

He opens his eyes. 'Yes, something's not right.'

'I didn't sleep at all. Is it the bed?'

We get out of bed and assess it — the same bed we've slept soundly on for years at the old house.

'Has it been put together wrong?' I think back to the stress of removal day. The removal team had started talking about clocking-off the minute they arrived. They'd obviously rushed it. 'Doesn't anyone take care in what they do anymore? If a job's worth doing, it's worth doing right.'

Chris looks under the bed, pulls off the mattress, checks the frame. 'Don't blame them. It's fine.'

'It's not. They've put it together wrong. We need to take it apart.' I look under the bed. 'There was more space under here before.'

'There can't have been.'

'There was. I know my bed!'

Chris looks again. 'It's been put together fine,' he says.

'It needs to be higher.'

'It won't go any higher.'

I check. It won't. I turn back to the wardrobe. 'Is that bigger then?'

'How?' Chris says, scratching his head.

We go downstairs, make a cup of tea. I call my dad and explain the current crisis. 'We're baffled.'

'I'll be right there,' he says. 'I've run out of jobs to do.'

Twenty minutes later, he and Mum arrive. 'Are we in your bubble?' Mum says. 'I don't want to give you germs when you've got asthma.'

'I don't care anymore,' I say, yawning. 'I just want a good

night's sleep.'

The four of us stand and stare at the bed. Dad confirms what Chris has already told me. 'The removal man has done a good job. It's fine. Nothing wrong with it.'

'It's not right,' I say.

'Are you sure?' Mum says.

'I'm not making it up. That bed feels wrong.'

'It can't do,' Dad says.

'It does.'

'Is the floor lower?' Mum says.

Slowly the three of us turn to my mother, who is kneeling on the floor, checking it.

'Have you really just said that?' I say.

'What?'

'The floor is the floor,' Dad says.

'Yes, but is it higher than the old floor?'

'How can the floor be higher or lower?' I say and then laugh so much, I don't think I will ever stop.

'There's no need to laugh,' Mum says. 'It's these tablets I'm taking — the amphetamines — they make me drowsy.'

'Antihistamines.'

Mum fixes her eyes on me. 'That's what I said.'

We investigate the bed again. We realise that there are two ways the bed sides could have been put together. The correct way — as they are now — and the incorrect way.

'Let's measure them,' Dad says.

Chris goes downstairs and returns with a tape measure. There is an inch difference between the correct and incorrect ways.

'I told you!' I say. 'I could tell. That inch made so much difference.'

'Yes,' Dad says. 'But whoever put that together the first time, did it completely wrong.'

'You did.'

'You supervised.'

'Hang on,' Chris says. 'So, for years, we've been sleeping on a bed that's not been right?'

'Yes,' Dad says.

'You'll have to take it apart and put it back together the wrong way,' Mum says. 'Or put up with it.'

Chris turns to me. 'If a job's worth doing, it's worth doing right,' he says. 'Isn't that what you say?'

'It is right,' Mum says. 'But she wants it the wrong way.'

'No,' I say. 'I really don't care anymore. I'm that tired, I'll sleep anywhere.'

27 June 2020

Flatpack hell

'We need to do something about your books,' Chris says, standing in the doorway to the spare room, afraid to step inside. 'You have too many.'

'There's no such thing as too many books.'

'They're everywhere.' He points to the piles of books stacked floor to ceiling and covering every inch of carpet.

'It's my book room,' I say, as though that explains everything. 'It's why we moved.'

'Yes, but they're taking over. It's just like the old book room. I can't get in!'

'It's not. You can.' At the old house, I'd crammed my library into a six-by-six box room. It was so bulging with books that the door wouldn't open, and I had to squeeze in sideways. Chris didn't even try.

'I'm worried they'll not fit,' he says. 'There's still boxes full in the garage.'

'We should have got a bigger house.'

'You'd just fill it with more books.' He shakes his head and sighs loudly. There is a strange look on his face. He looks like a man on the verge of a meltdown.

'What we need,' I say, taking charge, 'are emergency bookcases. To replace the ones that collapsed during the move.'

'What we need,' he says, 'is to get rid of some books.'

'No, we don't! Emergency bookcases will be fine, just something to get them off the floor so it at least looks tidy.'

'Where from?' he asks.

In normal times, I'd had a dream of floor-to-ceiling bookcases, made to measure, and with a ladder. We would have visited shops, browsed their bookcases, chosen ones we loved. I'm not a shopper, but I was looking forward to it.

In these coronavirus times, my bookcase dreams have been shattered, replaced with a flatpack reality.

'Anywhere,' I say, grabbing my phone and beginning the search.

Every shop I try is out of stock. 'It's the flour all over again,' I say. 'People have finished baking and are now sitting down enjoying a slice of cake and a good book.'

I eventually find some I sort-of like, but they are out of stock for delivery and will need to be clicked and collected from Birmingham.

'No,' Chris says before I've even suggested it.

I phone Mum to ask her shopping advice. Unlike me, she is a shopper, has continued to shop throughout the crisis and will not let anything stand in her shopping way.

'It needs to be online,' I say before she suggests a trip out.

'I wish you didn't have asthma,' she says. 'Then you could leave the house and shop.'

'Mum!'

'What about Ikea?' she suggests. 'They'll probably deliver.'

Sure enough, Ikea has a selection of Billy bookcases available for delivery. It's just that the cost of delivery is three times the price of the bookcases.

'How much!' Chris says when I tell him.

'It's that or Birmingham.'

While we're waiting for them to arrive, we move the books from the book room into another room so we can get in to put up the shelves.

'You need to be careful,' Mum says. 'Flatpacks cause divorce.'

'Don't be ridiculous,' I say. 'It's just a bookcase. It can't be that hard to put together.'

She smiles. 'Divorce or injury. Remember what happened the last time you were sorting your library?'

'How could I forget?' I'd spent hours in Accident and Emergency waiting to get my head looked at after a huge tome from the top shelf had fallen on my head. I'd been sitting on the floor alphabetising the bottom shelf and not seen it coming.

'There's no internal damage,' the doctor had told me. 'But you'll have a headache for a fortnight.'

'That's not going to happen again,' I say, and just to make sure I empty the existing bookcases before work begins on the new ones.

The bookcases arrive in two enormous boxes that we struggle to get upstairs. We open them and find hundreds of screws in little bags.

'Don't worry,' Chris says, glancing at the instructions. 'It's more straight-forward than it looks.'

'Are you sure?'

'Err…' He's already lifting planks of wood and joining them together. Within half an hour we have something resembling a frame.

'All we need to do is slot the back in,' he says. 'From the bottom to the top.'

And this is the problem, because the room is not big enough to do that. Unless we knock the walls down, we can't put them together like the instructions say. We stand and stare at the flatpack, unsure how to proceed.

And then I have an idea – to use more force. The back now slots into place. We lift the bookcase to its feet and manoeuvre it into position.

'It looks perfect,' I say. But there is no time for admiring our work. Chris is already starting on bookcase number two.

'You doubted me,' he says.

'I thought you were hopeless at DIY.'

We put bookcase two together in record time.

'Where's it going?' Chris asks.

'Where the smaller ones are.' I point to the existing bookcases. 'We'll need to move them first.'

He lifts one.

'Careful,' I say. 'They're not — '

But it's too late. The top shelf is already making its way towards his foot.

'Ahhhhh.' His face is pale, his eyes watering. He bends over and starts gulping in air.

I open the window. The couple next door are in their garden – him mowing the lawn, her painting the rabbit hutch – the picture of DIY bliss.

Behind me, Chris lets out another scream.

'You're being dramatic,' I want to say but I don't because his face looks deathly white, all the colour drained away.

He takes a deep breath. 'I think I've broken my toe.'

'Not the toe you broke in that fell race last year?'

'Yes.'

'It was only just starting to heal.'

'I know!'

I move closer to inspect the injury. Blood is pouring out.

'Don't bleed on my new carpet.' I pass him some tissue. His toe and foot are turning blue and swelling.

'Do you need to go to hospital?' I ask, not wanting to go near a hospital at all.

'I'm beginning to detest your passion for books,' he says, hobbling towards the door.

'The bookcases look good, though.' I follow him out, closing the door to the book room behind us.

4 July 2020

All insects great and small

'How's the new house?' my auntie asks when I meet her at the garden centre for a brew.

'It's still standing,' I say, thinking about the long snagging list that is getting longer by the day.

'That's what you get with new builds,' she tells me. 'One of my friends bought a new house, and it took two years to get it all sorted.'

'Two years!' My heart plummets at the thought.

'Worth the hassle though,' she says, smiling. 'Looks amazing now.'

I take a drink of my tea. I can't cope with another two years of what I can only describe as new-build hell.

'It's awful,' I tell her. 'They come to fix things but break something else. A man came to look at the bathroom floor and knocked the fence down. Another man came to repair the washing machine but ended up destroying it. Then another man came to replace the washing machine and wrecked the kitchen cupboards.'

'That's what happens,' she says, suddenly an expert in new-build homes. 'My friend had someone round to sort the shower. He fixed the leak but smashed the shower tray.'

I sigh, understanding exactly how her friend must have felt. 'It's never ending,' I say. 'It's like an endless cycle of destruction with no one taking any care.'

'And you've got standards,' she says.

'I just think, if a job's worth doing, it's worth doing right. Not botch it and run.'

'Yes.' She nods. 'Do you want some cake?'

Given the size of my hips, I should not be eating more cake, but it really helps. 'Just a sliver.'

My auntie approaches the counter where the woman serving is safely behind a floor-to-ceiling screen. There's a speaker connected to it, but my auntie doesn't realise this, and shouts her order so loud I'm sure they'll hear in the next village.

'Two slices of CHOCOLATE CAKE.'

'They'll bring it over.' She sits back down. 'Where were we?'

'The house,' I say, aware that my constant complaining does not make for interesting conversation, but I carry on anyway, happy to have someone to talk to. 'Everyone on the street has six spotlights in their kitchen, but not us. They only gave us four. The electrician wasn't good with numbers, apparently.'

'Shocking.' She takes a sip of her coffee, trying to hide her smile.

'It's not funny.' I laugh anyway.

'Are you being dramatic?' she asks.

'No, Chris feels the same.'

'Does he?'

I picture Chris's panicked face when he'd realised the workman had fixed the floor but knocked down the fence. 'When will this stop?' he'd wailed. 'It's just one thing after another.' It was a head-in-hands moment.

'Yes,' I say. 'He's had enough, too. They're incompetent. They never turn up when they say they will, and when they do, they breeze in with no masks or PPE as though coronavirus doesn't exist on building sites.'

'Now that is shocking.' And this time, her face is serious, not even a hint of a smile.

'I'm frazzled,' I tell her, because now I've started talking, I'm unable to stop. 'I've been working the day job, coping with a global pandemic, and project managing the rebuild of a new-build. I'm hovering on the edge.'

'Well, things can only get better.'

I shake my head. 'No. Just when I was thinking things couldn't get any worse, they started doing the road.'

'Was it loud?'

'Loud?! I had to work at my mum's. And I could still hear them ten miles away.'

She laughs. 'Could you concentrate with your mum talking all the time?'

'I can block her out. But the drilling... too high-pitched.'

The waitress emerges from behind the screen and places our slices of cake on the table. It's not just chocolate cake, but chocolate Guinness cake, and the portions are huge, not quite the sliver I'd hoped for.

The sponge is rich, soft and delicious, instantly making life seem better. 'This is good,' I say between mouthfuls.

In only a few seconds, my auntie has almost scoffed the lot. 'Amazing,' she says, looking over at the counter as if she's considering another slice. She puts down her fork and looks back to me.

'Don't worry, they're just minor snags, you'll get them sorted. You need to be positive and it will all come together.'

I take another bite of cake, and another. Three and a half months of living on a building site with the relentless drilling and hammering, not to mention coping with the builder's bodge-it approach, has sapped most of my positivity and strength.

I'm dreaming of the day when the builders move on to building pastures new. Hopefully, to somewhere far, far away, where they can cause as much construction chaos as they like.

'I've had enough,' I tell her. 'I spend my days wondering when the next disaster will strike.'

'That's no way to live,' she says, using her fork to scrape all the chocolate off her plate. 'Do you have any positives?'

'No.'

'Come on. There must be something.'

I take a while to think. 'We have blinds now. We've had cardboard curtains since we moved in. Everyone was buying blinds during lockdown, so there was a backlog.'

'That's wonderful. Not all doom and gloom.'

I smile. 'I quite liked the cardboard ones.'

She reaches out and touches me. A tender gesture, but I hope she's washed and disinfected her hands.

'Are you okay?' she says. 'I'm worried about you.'

I nod, blinking back the tears.

'You need to relax and start to enjoy the house.' She squeezes my hand. 'You need to enjoy every moment.'

That night, I tell Chris what she said.

'Enjoy it!' he says. 'We've not stopped since we moved in.'

'I know.'

He thinks for a second. 'We could cook a really nice dinner tomorrow night and then watch a film — maybe try to make it to the end of that Brad Pitt film.'

'Sounds like a plan.'

The next evening, Chris cooks and I help (by staying out of his way). We put on some music and because the weather's nice, we open the windows and patio doors. It's almost — but not quite — like being abroad.

The light fades quickly. One minute it's light, the next it's dark, but we leave the windows open, enjoying what's left of the summer, chatting and laughing and enjoying the house for the first time in months.

I lean back against my chair, and as I do, something moves behind Chris's head. There's another flicker to my left. I hear buzzing. And then a huge insect flies into Chris's face.

'Shut the windows,' I shout. 'We're under attack.'

Within seconds the room is full of insects, great and small. Some buzz straight at us, others hide in the corners or under the lights, casting dancing shadows on the walls.

'This never happened at the old house,' I say.

'We weren't on the top of a moor before. There's obviously a lot more nature about.'

'And it's all in our house!'

I pick up a book and swat at a fly. 'We'll never get a night to relax.'

Chris doesn't answer. He's trying but failing to outmanoeuvre a particularly bothersome flying friend.

It flutters into the kitchen, hovering in the corner of the ceiling. I pick up a tea towel, take aim and throw. It misses and lands on the top of the cupboard.

Chris laughs. 'Well, that's done the trick,' he says.

I pull up a chair and climb up to retrieve the tea towel, only to come face-to-face with a crater in the plasterboard. 'Look at this!'

Chris climbs up next to me and we stare into the hole. 'They probably didn't think we'd notice,' he says.

I take a picture and email the building firm, letting them

have my unfiltered thoughts about their slapdash workmanship. 'They didn't realise we'd spend an evening chasing flying insects and end up on top of the kitchen units. Nothing gets past me.'

Email sent, I return my attention to the insects.

They move quickly. But so do we. We spend the rest of the evening chasing them from one side of the room to the other. Just as we think we've got them all out, the big bothersome one makes a comeback. Chris lurches for it, but misses, almost falling over.

I can't help but laugh. I laugh so much that my shoulders shake, and tears stream down my face. Chris laughs too.

'Is this what she meant by enjoying the house?' he asks.

There's no time to answer. The creature settles on the wall.

'There!' I shout. 'Get it!'

26 September 2020

III

THE NEW NORMAL

Navigating the new normal

Stepping back out into society after months of lockdown was strange and terrifying and liberating all rolled into one.

At first, apart from the fact that I was significantly fatter, not much changed for me. I watched from the wings as friends and family threw themselves back into shopping and meals out and holidays and afternoon tea, making the most of life as best they could.

Having asthma, I was a little more tentative about taking those first steps. I managed a visit to York Marina, sitting outside and having breakfast on the blustery riverbank, then it was the garden centre, not once, not twice, but three times (rock 'n' roll!), then the dentist and the bookshop (on the same day), and then more bookshops. It's the bookshop visits that have kept me going.

Each time, I never left home without my Covid attack pack of mask, spare mask, sanitising wipes, spray and gloves. Even my sister did away with her designer handbags in favour of a Covid pack.

Life is strange.

In this section, I write about adjusting to life after lockdown, from first stepping onto the scales, to getting to grips with the track and trace system, to the joy of having a conversation with someone I wasn't related to for the first time in months. I hope you find them relatable and I hope they make you smile.

The Good Life

'I'm worried about your sister,' Mum tells me during one of our tea and cake chats in what was formerly the conservatory but is now known as the bubble.

'Why?' I say, taking a sip of my tea. 'What's wrong?'

'She's not herself. She's talking about getting some ducks.'

'Ducks?'

'Yes!'

'Real ones?'

'Yes. Living and breathing and quacking ones.'

I study Mum's face, trying to work out if she's serious or not. She cuts a large slice of cake and hands it to me. Her face is etched with worry.

'But she doesn't do the outdoors,' I say.

She cuts an equally large slice of cake for herself. 'I don't know where it's come from. This lockdown has done strange things. First you with your cleaning and now her with her feathered friends.'

I take another sip of tea, trying to imagine my glamorous sister in wellies, mucking out a duck house. 'I just can't see it.'

'Exactly,' Mum says. 'Handbags yes. Ducks no.'

'She just wanted to get back to usual shopping life,' I say, remembering an incident a few months into lockdown when my sister had phoned me in a distressed state. 'For the sake of my sanity,' she'd said, 'I need to shop. It's what I do. I shop!'

'But she can shop now,' I say to Mum. 'So, what's with the ducks?'

Mum shakes her head, looks forlornly out of the window. 'I don't know what the world's coming to.'

'Maybe she's embracing the Good Life,' I say.

'Does she think she's Felicity Kendal?'

I smile. 'She's more Margo.'

Later that night, my sister phones. 'Has Mum told you? We've ordered some ducks.'

'That's lovely,' I say. 'What kind?'

'They're ducks,' she says.

'I know, but what breed?'

The line goes quiet.

'There are different breeds,' I say, thinking the only duck she's ever ordered before came with pancakes and hoisin sauce.

'I'll phone you back,' she says.

I sit waiting for her call, worried that she's ordered geese by mistake. I imagine them hissing and spitting at my sister and niece.

A few minutes later, she's back on the phone. 'Indian Runner Ducks. They're like penguins, but not. They do the waddle thing.'

'Ah,' I say, already desperate to meet them. 'They'll be lovely.'

'Dad's going to build them a house,' she says.

Work on the duck house begins immediately, taking every hour of every day. Dad goes early and returns late, each time looking more and more exhausted.

'Why's it taking so long?' I ask, beginning to worry that the duck house could be the undoing of my dad.

'This isn't an ordinary duck house,' Mum says. 'This is your sister's duck house. It's huge.'

That night I dream of a duck house like the bird cage in *Jurassic Park*, but the ducks are not ducks at all. They are velociraptors. After that, whenever the duck house is mentioned, I get an uneasy feeling.

Just as the duck build is nearing completion, with pond, steps, sunbathing spot and patio area, I get another call from my sister.

'Rabbits,' she says. 'Should we get some rabbits?'

'Yes.'

'They're expensive. A hundred and fifty for two.'

'How much?'

'But they're hard to get hold of since lockdown and they're lovely.'

She sends a picture.

'Ah,' I say, immediately falling in love. 'They're cute.' I turn the phone to show Chris. 'They're getting rabbits.'

'If she wants encouragement to buy an animal, she's phoned the right person,' he says.

'I know. She did it with the horse. The horse that thirteen years later, I'm still looking after.'

'It's exciting,' she says. 'And my ducks are coming soon. It'll be like a farm.'

'It'll be great.' I'm so excited about the new arrivals.

A week later, I get another call. 'We have rabbits,' she says. 'But they were one hundred and fifty each.'

'Each! You could have had mine for free.'

'Well, we've not been shopping,' she says. 'Or been anywhere, really, so we bought them.'

I am secretly pleased because I am desperate to cuddle a baby rabbit.

'Are you coming to meet them?' she says.

When I arrive, Dad is still working on the duck house and Mum is supervising. My sister is in her wellies, mucking out the rabbits.

'You know the shops are open,' I tell her.

She stops shovelling rabbit poo and smiles. 'I know but this is fun.'

I look at Mum; Mum looks at me.

'The Good Life,' I say.

18 July 2020

The scales don't lie

It is nine o'clock on Saturday morning, sixteen weeks and six days since lockdown began, when I finally stop procrastinating and step onto the scales.

I stand as tall as I can, willing myself thinner. It takes a few seconds for the scales to give their verdict. In those few seconds, I hold my breath and close my eyes, and all the cakes and chocolate and biscuits that I've devoured in lockdown flash through my mind.

It is an obscene amount of food. I have no choice but to face up to the grim reality. I look down and there it is — the number I've been dreading. And just to make sure I don't miss it, it flashes.

I step off the scales, reposition them on a different tile, and step back on. I'm a quarter of a pound heavier, so I try again. A pound heavier, gaining weight at rapid speed. On the fourth attempt, I'm the same weight as the first reading. It will have to do.

'Is it bad?' Chris asks, coming up behind me.

'Well... yes.'

The number is still flashing. I wish it would stop. Chris sees it and grimaces.

'Ouch,' he says.

'Maybe it's the floor,' I say. 'It's different from the one at the old house. It could cause the scales to read heavier.'

He shakes his head. 'The scales don't lie.'

'I'm fat!'

'You're not fat.'

'I am. People keep telling me how well I look. They only ever do that when I've gained weight.'

'You can lose it.' Chris has developed an annoyingly positive voice. 'You've done it before.'

I sigh. I have and I know exactly how much energy, effort and willpower it takes. And, in recent weeks, my reserves of energy, effort and willpower have been exhausted.

'I don't have the energy or willpower,' I say.

'That's the spirit.'

'It's all right for you, you're not fat. Why aren't you fat? You've been stuffing your face, too.'

'I've been going on the bike.'

'So have I.'

'Once,' he says.

'Twice.'

I put the scales in the cupboard and go downstairs, ashamed that I've done this to myself. My exercise sessions have been sporadic. My eating of cake has been consistent. For the foreseeable future, my life will involve less of one and more of the other.

'Exactly how big are you?' Mum asks later that day when we're sitting at her kitchen table with a brew but without biscuits or cake.

'Ten stone, two and a half.'

She gasps. 'That's a lot for you.'

'I know!'

'What were you on your wedding day?'

'Eight stone, thirteen and a half.'

'Blimey, you've really piled it on.'

I take a drink of my tea and say nothing.

'Ten stone.' Mum shakes her head, as though she still can't believe it. She turns to Chris. 'You haven't put any on, have you?'

'Can we change the subject?' I say.

'Biscuit anyone?' Dad says, breezing into the kitchen and taking a digestive from the cupboard.

'No!' Mum and I shout.

She turns to me. 'Could you try to lose a few pounds for your birthday?'

'Not enough time.'

I take another sip of tea, and watch Dad eat his biscuit, then go back for another.

'This time last year, I was young and thin and in Crete,' I tell them. 'Now I'm old and fat and here. I wish I'd done a Shirley Valentine with that lovely Greek waiter.'

'That would have been good for Chris,' Dad says.

'Good for everyone,' Chris says.

Mum nods. 'Greece hasn't had many cases of coronavirus.'

'Win-win,' I say.

'We're worried about you.' Mum looks serious. 'You've been doing too much. You need to relax and put yourself back together. Get the old you back.'

'I'm frazzled,' I say. Over the past few months — a house move, a day job, home-working with the husband, looking after horses and dogs and rabbit, trying to achieve my dream of becoming a best-selling author, or even just an author, and coping with the world in its current state — have all sent my stress levels soaring.

'We'd noticed. But you're already looking better. A few pounds off and you'll be back to normal.'

That night, I think about what I need to do to lose the extra few pounds. I remember all the things I used to do before lockdown like running and spinning and strength classes. And how they balanced out the chocolate and cake.

For the rest of the weekend, I continue eating at the lockdown levels my body has become accustomed to. I devour one last slice of cake and then follow it with another because it's delicious.

The diet begins on Monday, fails Tuesday and restarts on Wednesday. Thursday is a success, followed by another good day on Friday. By the weekend, I have some momentum.

I feel strong and positive that I can scrape some effort and willpower from somewhere. I can be fit and healthy again. I will be fit and healthy again.

'The recovery begins,' Mum says. 'You can do it.'

'I'm on it. And when I'm back to normal, we'll go for afternoon tea to celebrate.'

1 August 2020

It's my birthday and I'll cry if I want to

'We need to do something for your birthday,' Chris says, the day before I turn forty-one.

'This time last year, we were in Crete,' I say.

'I know.'

'We had that meal looking out to sea, and that amazing chocolate pudding.'

'The grill pit,' Chris says. 'I ended up having to cook at the table.'

'And Olivia FaceTimed to sing happy birthday.'

Chris smiles. 'She was in Turkey and said she could hear us across the water.'

'The entire day was perfect.' It had made turning forty bearable.

We'd been into Agios Nikolaos during the day, had lunch and drinks and ice cream, and seen the statue of Europa, then strolled around the shops. Chris said that if I saw anything I fancied, he would treat me as an extra birthday present. But when I'd spotted a beautiful 5,000-euro bracelet with matching chain and earrings (also 5,000 euros each), he'd changed his mind.

I sigh. 'If only I'd known then what would happen to the world, I wouldn't have had a meltdown about turning forty.'

'Probably best not to know.'

'Forty seemed momentous,' I say. 'Now I'm on the cusp of forty-one, it's young. And it seems such a long time ago.'

I stare out of the kitchen window, take a drink of tea, remembering the happy times of my youth.

'I'd decided that forty was going to be a fun year and the start of a fun decade. All about fun. It's not working out quite how I'd hoped.'

'We can have fun,' Chris says, nodding enthusiastically like he's trying to convince himself. 'What would you like to do?'

'Go to Crete and buy that expensive jewellery.'

A look of panic flashes across his face. 'What about a meal out?'

'No!' Now it's my turn to panic. 'I'm not ready for that yet.'

'Something round here, then.'

'Somewhere without people,' I say. 'Somewhere tolerant of unruly dogs, because they'll have to come too. And somewhere nearby, so we'll not have to use public toilets.'

We sit and think. 'A mission to Mars would be easier,' I say, making us another brew.

While I'm waiting for the kettle to boil, inspiration strikes. 'Holmfirth!'

'What about it?'

'We can go. And walk and take a picnic. It'll be great.'

'Sounds like a plan.' Chris looks relieved.

On the morning of my birthday, I go downstairs to make a cup of tea. I stand in the kitchen with the sunlight streaming in, enjoying a moment of calm.

I take time to notice my surroundings because that's what mindfulness is all about. And after all the chaos, I'm trying to be more mindful. I look around the kitchen. And that's when I spot the scratches on the new floor — under Chris's chair. It's like someone has taken a knife and repeatedly stabbed it into the floor.

'Chris!'

He comes downstairs. 'Happy birthday,' he says. 'It's early.'

I point to the floor. 'Look what you've done!'

He crouches down to investigate. 'How's this happened?'

'You,' I say. 'It's your fault. Scraping your chair.' I go to my side of the table. There are no scratches anywhere.

'The new floor,' he says, looking like he might cry.

'Yes, the new floor! You've ruined it.' And that's when my tears start. I know it is only a floor and there are much more upsetting things going on in the world, but suddenly it's the worst thing ever and my husband is a chair-scraping monster, and surely this is grounds for divorce.

'Don't cry,' he says. 'It's your birthday.'

'Yes! It's my birthday. And look what you've done.' I storm out of the room, turning back to shout. 'And I'll cry if I want to.'

Upstairs, I stand in the shower and sob, letting the hot water wash away my rage. It's the first time I've had a good cry in ages. I cry and cry and cry, my tears mixing with the water. I can't help but wonder how a bit of laminate could provoke such a reaction. When I step out, I feel better — revived, almost.

'I've made a picnic,' Chris says when I go downstairs. 'Are we still going?'

'Yes. I don't want to stay here and keep looking at the floor.'

We drive in silence, park in the car park next to the Co-op. Chris struggles to squeeze the car into a tight spot. I take a deep breath and then another.

He turns the engine off. 'I'm sorry about the floor,' he says. 'I didn't mean to destroy it.'

'You're a liability,' I say.

'I'll sort it.'

'How?' The upset I'd felt about the floor is immediately replaced with a worry about Chris's DIY skills and just how he intends to 'sort it'.

'I Googled it when you were in the shower. WD-40 could help.'

'No,' I say, my heart rate rocketing. 'Promise me you'll not put WD-40 anywhere near that floor.'

'It might help.'

'No,' I say, firmly. 'We'll get a mat.'

And with that decision, I open the car door and step out into society for the first time since March.

The first thing I notice are the people — lots of them — scurrying around, masks on, heads down. It's like the sleepy town of Holmfirth has turned into a sprawling metropolis.

The second thing I notice are the panicked glances, people crossing over roads to avoid getting within a few metres of anyone else.

I take the little dog and begin speed-walking out of town. 'It's too people-y,' I shout over my shoulder. 'I'm heading for the hills.'

Chris and the big dog walk behind, struggling to keep up.

The first hill is huge, and I wish I'd invested in a pair of crampons.

Mum phones when I'm halfway up, sweating and out of breath.

'Happy birthday,' she says. 'Are you having a good day?'

'Well, I've only cried once.'

'That's good.' She laughs. 'Forty-one! Who would have thought I'd have a daughter so old?'

'I'm up a hill,' I say. 'In Holmfirth.'

'You've gone out? That's wonderful. I'll leave you to it.'

She hangs up, and I return to focusing on the climb. At the top, there's a water crossing with slippery stepping stones to navigate. The little dog hops across and I tiptoe behind.

After that, there's another hill and another and another. I focus on putting one foot in front of the other. With each step, I feel better. The stress of the floor crisis, and the house move and the snagging list and the virus and work and everything else that has been pushing me to the edge these past few weeks and months, eases.

My mind clears.

We reach the trig point and sit and eat our picnic, looking down on the world below. I turn to my husband and hounds.

'This is fun,' I say.

15 August 2020

Down by the river

'We need a day out.' Mum phones to tell me. 'We need to go out and eat something. All of us. We've not had a meal out since March.'

'Where do you want to go?'

'Somewhere outside. It has to be outside. I'm not doing the indoors anymore.'

I look out of the window. The sun is shining, and it's already hot. I've heard on the radio it's going to be the hottest day of the year. Thirty degrees. Eating outdoors is a great idea.

'We could go to York Marina,' I say. 'We can sit outside at the café overlooking the river.' In my mind, I'm already there, relaxing on the riverbank, drink in hand.

'What time shall we pick you up?'

'Not today,' Mum says. 'Your dad's got his list of jobs. He's clearing out the shed and sorting the patio.'

'Oh.' I can't help but feel disappointed. 'When then?'

'Tomorrow,' she says, her voice bright. 'It's something to look forward to.'

When tomorrow comes, I hear the rain before I see it, lashing against the window. The temperature plummets and the heating kicks in.

Mum phones before I'm even out of bed.

'Are we cancelling?' I ask.

'No,' she says. 'Layer-up. We'll be fine with big coats and umbrellas.'

'Really?' My mum is not usually the outdoorsy type.

'We need a day out,' she says, sounding almost desperate. 'Are you ready? We'll need to leave early to miss the crowds.'

I'm not sure many people will head for the riverbank on a rainy day, but I get up and get ready, determined to have a rare and enjoyable family day out.

Within half an hour, we have dogs and parents in the car and are on our way. Rain splatters the windscreen.

Chris looks at his phone. 'It should stop raining in York at ten o'clock,' he informs us. 'It's better weather the further east we go.'

'We're going north,' I say.

'Well, it will only be slightly better.'

'Have you got that thing for Archie?' Dad asks. 'To shut him up when he barks?'

From the back of the car, Archie barks.

'Yes,' I say. 'But it's not on yet.'

'What is it?' Mum asks.

'An anti-bark collar,' I tell her. 'If he tries to bark, it'll squirt citrus. The smell distracts him.'

'So, he'll be quiet?'

Archie lets out another bark.

'In theory, yes.'

'As long as we don't run out of citronella spray,' Chris says, shaking the bottle.

'That's wonderful,' Mum says.

'Get it switched on,' Dad says.

When we pull into the car park, the torrential rain is easing, becoming more of a drizzle, but it's blustery by the river.

'They have a marquee.' Mum points to a bit of fabric flapping in the wind. It has no sides, but it has a roof. 'It's something,' she says, speed-walking towards it, on a mission to get the best seats in the house.

'Get back!' A woman comes out of nowhere, waving her arms. 'You've crossed the line. Go back. Go back.'

Mum looks startled but rushes to the right side of the line — a one metre bit of masking tape on the floor.

Archie pulls at his lead, growling at the woman.

'I need your details,' she growls back.

I step forward, making sure I do not cross the line. I open my mouth expecting the numbers to roll off my tongue, but my mind goes blank. '0778... Sorry, no, it's 0788...'

The woman glances at her watch.

I turn to Chris. 'What's my number?'

'I don't know.'

I have another attempt. 'That's definitely it,' I say, not sure at all.

She writes it down.

'Don't you know your number?' Mum says, shaking her head and giving a disapproving look, like I'm going to bring the entire track and trace system to its knees.

We take a table under the marquee, looking out at the murky waters of the River Ouse.

'I hope I've given the right number. Should I go back and check?'

'No!' Mum shouts. 'You can't cross that line. You can't go back.'

In my mind, I go over the number. 'I think it was okay... She put me on the spot, one question too many for a Sunday morning.'

The woman returns to take our order. Archie barks and the collar squirts citronella. It's strong stuff. He shuts up.

We eat our breakfast without a sound from either of the dogs. They curl up at our feet like they're the best-behaved dogs in the world.

'Aren't they good,' Dad says, sounding surprised.

'Don't speak too soon,' I say. 'There are no other dogs here yet. That's the real test.'

I sit back in my chair and watch the world go by. Lots of people are dressed in blue, with nautical-themed clothing. 'They're all very boaty people,' I say. 'It's like *Howards' Way*.'

'It is a boatyard,' Dad says. 'There's Tom.'

'Tom! We're going to lose the boatyard,' I say. 'Wasn't that the gist of every episode?' But there is a Tom, and Dad is on his feet, rushing over to greet him.

'Look at him,' Mum says. 'He loves coming here.'

Dad is nodding and smiling. Whenever he's near a river, he comes over all sociable, chatting to everyone like he's the captain of a cruise ship. Usually he doesn't say much at all. Anything, really.

'He's too close to that man,' Mum says, nudging me with her elbow. 'It's not two metres.'

Dad is practically embracing Tom. 'He needs to back off.'

He returns to the table and we tell him off for his recklessness and order another round of tea.

'Isn't this lovely?' Mum says, and just as the words are out, another dog strolls into the café. Archie spots it and barks three times. The collar gives three squirts of citronella. He licks his lips and shuts up.

'Good boy,' I tell him, feeling for once like a proud dog owner.

Just as the tea is arriving, another dog arrives and then another. Citronella bursts from the collar. It quietens the dog, but my chest is tightening — aerosols and perfumes trigger my asthma. I have an overwhelming urge to cough. I daren't. Not in public. Not in the middle of a pandemic. I hold it in, my eyes burning with the effort. Or maybe it's the citronella, I can't be sure.

More dogs and dog owners arrive. A labrador, a spaniel, a poodle. With each new arrival, Archie gets more and more excited. Our supplies of citronella are quickly diminishing. When he spots a shih-tzu, supplies are out.

Without the chastising scent of citronella, he barks and barks and barks. Most people pretend not to notice, a few send disapproving looks our way.

Chris grabs the dog and takes him to the side of the river. For a minute, I think both might jump in, but they sit down. Chris takes the spray from his pocket and refills the collar.

When they return, the dog is slightly less stressed. Chris is shaking. 'He's really wound up,' he says.

'It'll be fine,' I tell him. 'Finish your tea.'

And it is fine for about a minute. But the arrival of not one but two French bulldogs is too much excitement for Archie to bear. He loses it completely and the little dog, who has been curled up under my chair, joins in.

A cloud of citronella bursts from the collar, engulfing us. The strong scent overpowers my lungs. I cough and cough and cough. I feel everyone's eyes burning into me.

'We need to leave,' Dad says, jumping to his feet.

I take a long drink of tea, trying to stop the coughing. 'It's not coronavirus,' I want to shout. 'Asthma.' But I'm coughing too much to speak. I grab the dogs and do the walk of shame out of the café garden.

Archie doesn't bark at all. He trots along next to me, stopping briefly to lift his leg and wee on the menu board.

We make it back to the car, just as the rain lashes down again.

'What a lovely morning out,' Mum says.

'Traumatic,' I say. 'None of us have socialised since March. Us or the dogs. We're all rusty.'

'We've done well,' Mum says. 'Haven't we?'

Archie barks and wags his tail.

We drive home in silence, the smell of citrus lingering in the air.

29 August 2020

Woman-about-town

For the first time in five months, three weeks and two days, there's somewhere I need to be. It's written in the diary.

Thursday 27th August — dentist, 9.30am.

I start looking forward to it on Monday, planning what I'll wear and where I'll park and what I'll take with me (mask, hand sanitiser, wipes). It's like I've never had a day out.

'Why are you so excited about a trip to the dentist?' Chris asks.

'Because I'm going out on my own — without dogs, husband or parents. It's liberating.'

He nods and smiles, not quite understanding.

In normal times, my diary is fuller. There'd be work (in an actual office) and visits to bookshops, and cups of tea and slices of cake in various cafés. Since coronavirus came along, the only thing in my calendar has been the monthly reminder to deflea the dogs. To have to be somewhere is momentous.

'You're happy,' Mum says. 'What's wrong?'

'I'm going to the dentist.'

'Well, that's lovely. You're usually nervous.'

'Not anymore.' There's not even the hint of a nerve.

'Be careful,' she tells me. 'There's a pandemic on.'

'Is there?'

'You'll need to be organised and on time. Or they'll not let you in.'

'Mum, I'm forty-one.'

'I know. I'm just saying. You're never organised.'

The evening before my big day out, in an attempt to be organised, I download a car parking app. I don't want to be touching the ticket machine — that's a risk in life I'm not prepared to take.

And on the day of the appointment, I leave early. There is no last-minute panic, no having to wind the car window down to dry my hair because I'm late. I arrive feeling calm and in control.

I park on the edge of the car park and put ninety minutes on the app. A traffic warden saunters from car to car. He keeps glancing my way.

'I've paid,' I want to shout, but don't. Instead, I pretend I haven't noticed him, hoping that somehow my technology is talking to his technology.

'Where's your ticket?' he asks, coming towards my car.

'I paid on the app.' I raise my voice so he can hear me through the closed window.

He shakes his head. 'It's not come up.'

He moves to the front of the car, looks from number plate to his hand-held device, and starts typing in my registration. He continues shaking his head. 'No, no, not here.'

Eventually he nods. 'Got it!' he says.

I smile, grateful that I will not be branded a car parking thief and fined a hefty sum. I wait until he's moved to the next row of cars, then I scramble out, ready to take my tentative first steps back into society.

At the dentist, I can only enter at the exact time of my appointment. Not too early. Not too late. I stand on the pavement with my mask on, watching the seconds on my watch tick by.

At half past, I tap on the glass. The masked receptionist opens the door. I step into a square marked out with blue tape while she holds a thermometer to my head.

It's a hot day. I've been sitting in the car with the windows up. I've had the stress of the traffic warden. I worry that my temperature will have rocketed, but it appears I am normal and allowed to enter.

She offers me a seat on a plastic chair, but I daren't move or talk or even breathe. My heart is thudding. This isn't a good idea. I have to leave. Just as I'm turning to run for the safety of the car, a woman calls me upstairs.

I do not touch the bannister. I do not touch the door handles. I'm asked to place all my belongings, including mask, into a plastic box. I worry about touching it. But I do, and then take a seat in the chair.

The dentist is in a mask and visor. Without my mask, I feel barely dressed.

'Are you okay?' she asks, coming closer. 'It's all very strange, takes some getting used to.'

As she reclines the chair, she places her hand on my shoulder. After months of people scurrying away from each other in fear, this human contact and kindness almost makes me cry.

'It's awful,' I say. 'I still can't believe it's happening.'

She nods, and as she does, I realise that I've not had a face-to-face conversation with anyone other than my family since this dreadful thing began. I have an overwhelming urge to chat. And so does the dentist.

'What are you doing for the rest of the day?' she says.

'Visiting the bookshop,' I tell her. 'I'm so excited.'

'That's great,' she says. 'Have you read *The Tattooist of Auschwitz*?'

'Not yet, but my friend just bought it for me for my birthday.'

'I read it in a day,' she tells me. 'You should read it.'

We talk about how lockdown helped her rediscover her love of reading, and then we move on to flossing and tooth brushing. I ask lots of questions and buy some toothbrushes.

With all the chat, the appointment is longer than expected, and the parking app is ticking. There's not long left, but it's enough to walk into town and back.

Visiting a bookshop has been on my mind for ages, but I've kept it to myself, knowing that my mum would say it's too dangerous — I should be shielding and not risking my life for a book. But I have missed the simple pleasure of browsing in a bookshop more than anything.

With gel and wipes in my pocket, I set off into town. Barnsley is not busy by usual standards, but it is busy by coronavirus standards. I speed-walk towards the shop, zigzagging to avoid the shoppers.

I've not been to this bookshop before (it's new) but I know where it is — on the corner of Market Street next to Pinocchio's Italian. Except it's not there. I look around, wondering if it's gone out of business. These are strange and stagnant times. Anything could have happened. I grab my phone and check. It is still in business. It is still on Market Street. It's me who's in the wrong place.

I consult my phone for directions, but it thinks I'm in the United States. I consider asking someone, but they might think I'm riddled with disease and run away. I'll have to rely on my instincts. Barnsley is not a big place. It has to be around here somewhere. I look at my watch. Twenty-five minutes until my car parking runs out.

I cover most of the town centre, but there is no sign of a bookshop. More and more shoppers dart this way and that, struggling to maintain any distance. No one makes eye contact.

I'm surrounded by so many people but feel lost and alone. I need to get back to the car. But just as I'm turning, I have a flicker of a memory. It's of me at eighteen, moving to London and not knowing anyone. I wasn't afraid in the slightest and fell in love with the hustle and bustle of the city. If I can do that, then I can navigate Barnsley town centre at forty-one.

I resume my speed-walking. There is one road left — at the back of M&S. I don't know what it's called. I turn a corner and bump straight into an unmasked man just as he's shouting to someone.

Startled, I leap out of his way, and that's when I see it.

The Book Vault.

I race towards it, step inside, and breathe in the wonderful smell of books.

The place is a sanctuary of calm. I amble around the shop, looking at fiction, non-fiction and the latest releases, my stress and panic easing. I do another lap and select two titles I've wanted for a while. I'm heading to the desk to pay when a bright cover grabs my attention. I pick it up and read the blurb. I'm not sure about book-browsing etiquette. If I touch, do I have to buy? If I put it back, and have the virus, could I be putting others at risk? It's best for everyone if I buy it.

'That's a fantastic read,' the bookseller tells me. 'Really funny.'

I smile and, for the second time in a morning, have a conversation with someone I'm not related to.

Being in a bookshop, talking about books makes life seem almost normal again. I could stay all day, but... the car!

Three minutes until my ticket runs out and the traffic warden pounces.

I stuff my books into my bag and run.

12 September 2020

The rule of six

'Do not get me anything with seventy written on it,' Mum says. 'I don't want to be reminded.'

'It's your birthday,' I say.

'I don't want a fuss.'

'You do.'

'I don't.'

I sigh. Whenever we mention anything about her forthcoming big birthday, the conversation always goes the same way. No to balloons. No to a party. No to anything with seventy written on it.

'What shall we do?' my sister, Sarah, asks, the worry showing on her face.

'Take no notice.' I use my big-sister-I-know-best voice. 'She doesn't mean it. We're making a fuss of her. And she'll love it.'

'Are you sure?'

'No. But we need to do something.'

Planning begins immediately. We consult government guidelines to see how many people we can invite. We send out the invites. We ring the guests to confirm. We order balloons and banners and bunting. Everything we buy has a seven and a zero written on it.

The next thing to decide is the present. 'How about pooling our money and getting her some jewellery?' I suggest.

Sarah agrees. Dad agrees. 'Let me know what I owe you,' he says. 'But remember, I'm a pensioner.'

In a normal world, my sister and I would go to a jewellery store together, take our time, maybe have some lunch. Afterwards Sarah would buy a handbag, and I'd buy a book. But as there is nothing normal about the world, we have a rethink.

'You order online,' Sarah says. 'And I'll go to Meadowhall to collect it.'

This seems like a good plan, but the next day she calls me back. 'Can you get it delivered instead?' She sighs. 'I was going to do some shopping when I went to pick it up, but shopping's not an enjoyable experience anymore.'

It is at this moment — when my shopaholic sister is turning down a shopping trip — that I realise the world has changed beyond recognition. 'Are you sure?'

'Yes.' Her voice is flat. 'It's not fun anymore.'

I am not a shopper, have never been a shopper, but I feel an overwhelming sadness for my sister who has lost one of her main hobbies in life. Not to mention the economy. Without her shopping sprees, it's in for some turbulent times.

'Make sure you keep shopping online,' I say.

'I will.'

I get off the phone, picturing how happy she always looked coming out of a store with a new purchase. I think of our last shopping trip at Christmas, and how she went from shop to shop, eyes lighting up, never tiring, while I trailed behind, desperate to get to the bookshop and go home. I long for a return to those days.

Between us, we select something special for Mum. I order online but when I try to arrange delivery, the website doesn't recognise my postcode. It doesn't believe my new house exists. So I arrange delivery to Mum and Dad's house. I know this is risky, but they'll give me a delivery time so Dad can take it in without Mum even noticing. I wouldn't want her opening her present, or even seeing it, before her big day.

The order is going to plan. I get regular updates about its status. On Sunday evening, I receive an email saying it's out for delivery and will get a time slot tomorrow. This is good; everything is going to plan.

Until the next morning. At six o'clock, I receive a text message: the driver is on his way and will arrive in twenty minutes.

Twenty minutes!

I pick up the phone, call home, but there is no answer. They'll be in bed. And if the driver knocks on the door, it'll be Mum who wakes up first. I imagine her standing on the doorstep, looking at the parcel. 'I wonder what this is?' And she'll tear off the packaging. All our planning will have been for nothing.

I throw on some clothes, dive into the car *Dukes of Hazzard* style, and set off on the twenty-minute journey to my parents' house. I imagine how cross Sarah will look when I tell her I've ruined the surprise. Just the thought makes me hit the accelerator hard.

I arrive just after the delivery man. He's walking up the drive, lifting his hand to knock on the door. In a second, I'm out of the car and running after him. 'Stop!'

I wrestle the package from him, just as Mum is opening the curtains. 'What are you doing?' she shouts through the window.

'Nothing,' I say.

It is twenty past six in the morning. I am standing half-dressed on my parents' front lawn with a man I've never met and a package I'm trying to hide behind my back.

'Cup of tea?' she says.

With the present safely delivered, plans for the party continue. Sarah orders the food, I sort the cake. Everything is ready to give Mum the wonderful day she deserves. Everything.

Just before I'm going to bed on Tuesday night, a news update comes through on my phone. 'Social gatherings over six to be banned in England.'

I stare at the article, checking the dates and guidelines. For a moment, I feel like putting my head in my hands and sobbing.

110

But I don't. I pull myself together and call my sister. 'We need to do the party on a smaller scale,' I tell her. 'The government says so.'

'How small?'

'Six people.'

'Six?'

'Six!'

'Right.'

'Mum will probably prefer a small gathering,' I say. 'She's never been one for big parties.'

We pick up the phone and start uninviting the guests, but the food and cake can't be unordered.

'We'll just have to eat a lot,' Sarah says, reeling off the list of food. 'Pizza, quiches, sandwiches, and puddings and party food for a small army.'

On the day of the birthday, we decorate the house, and jump out and shout 'Surprise!' With only five of us, it's not quite the same, but it's more than enough.

Mum smiles. 'I knew you were up to something. But I didn't expect all this.' She stands in front of the food, looking slightly overwhelmed.

'We were expecting a few more people,' I say. 'I hope you're hungry.'

17 October 2020

Bakewell tart, anyone?

'Bakewell tarts,' Dad says when I answer the phone.

'What about them?'

'I've made some.'

'For us?'

'Yes. Can you pick them up? Before I eat them all.'

I promise I'll be straight round and hang up. 'Chris,' I shout downstairs to where my husband is hard at work. 'Stop what you're doing. There's cake.'

Within minutes, we're in the car and on our way.

Under government tier two guidelines, we are no longer allowed inside my parents' house. But outdoor gatherings are still permitted. We can hover on the doorstep with a brew and a Bakewell tart.

As soon as we step out of the car, I get a whiff of home baking.

'Something smells good,' I say, opening the door but not going in.

Mum is sitting at the kitchen table with a book and a coffee. Dad is in front of the oven, taking out a batch of freshly baked scones.

'Scones as well?' I say.

He smiles and lifts the tray. 'Bakewell and scones.'

'He's been at it all afternoon,' Mum says, not looking up from her book. 'He's baking every day. He thinks he's one of the Hairy Bikers.'

'If it helps him cope. It's fine.'

Dad is baking his way through lockdown. It started in March with a batch of basic buns, before progressing to a plain and simple Victorian sponge. Then, in the summer, came the apple pie.

The tree he'd planted back in 2006 finally started blooming. So, he's been making apple pie after apple pie after apple pie. Each one was sweet, sticky, delicious and tasted better and better.

As autumn arrived and the last apples fell from the tree, his attention turned to scones. He found an old recipe of my grandmother's in a drawer. They're the best scones I've ever tasted (and I've had a few).

He bakes. We eat. All of us are getting fatter, but life is sweeter with one of his latest bakes to look forward to. And now we have the exciting addition of a Bakewell tart.

'I didn't think you liked Bakewell tart,' I say to Mum.

She puts her book down and screws up her face in disgust. 'I don't.'

Last year, for Mother's Day, we'd bought her a Bakewell tart afternoon tea in Bakewell. It wasn't until we were sitting at the table about to be served with Bakewell tart and Bakewell pudding, that she mentioned she didn't like anything Bakewell.

'It brings back bad memories of Granny Maud,' she said. 'She used to force feed us Bakewell tarts.'

I turned to my mother. 'We've bought you a Bakewell extravaganza and come all the way to Bakewell... Why didn't you say?'

'Well, I try not to think about it. She was quite mean.'

I'd heard the stories about Granny Maud, the woman her grandfather had married after the death of her real grandmother. But the Bakewell incidents had been blocked out, too traumatic to mention.

To save the afternoon tea experience, I'd eaten Mum's Bakewells, and she'd had my cakes. There was no tart trauma for me. I'd devoured the lot.

'Bakewell tart, anyone?' Dad lifts it from the cooling rack and cuts into it. Steam rises. 'It probably needs more time to cool.'

'No,' I say. 'It'll be fine.' It's getting chilly standing on the doorstep.

'Not yet,' he says. 'Have a scone first.'

I smother one in jam and cream and savour every mouthful. And then it's time for the main event, the Bakewell.

We sit on the garden bench and start eating.

Dad stands in the kitchen like a contestant on *The Great British Bake Off*, nervously awaiting our verdict. 'I couldn't find the Mary Berry recipe, so I used one off the internet... I wasn't sure about it... What do you think?'

'Delicious,' Chris says.

I nod and keep eating. The taste of almonds, the jam, the sponge, the crumbliness of the pastry is just amazing.

'The best thing you've made so far,' I say quickly between mouthfuls. If touching was allowed, I'd reach out and shake his hand, Paul Hollywood style. But that is against the rules. Instead, I shovel in the rest of the slice, devouring it in seconds.

'I didn't realise I was so hungry.' I stare into the kitchen at the rest of the tart, but just as I'm thinking of having another slice, my bottom lip starts tingling. Within moments, it's swelling. It feels like something is stuck at the back of my throat. I cough but can't dislodge it.

116

Dad gets a glass of water for me. But it's still there. My lip is getting bigger, my throat tighter.

'She's having an allergic reaction!' There is panic in Mum's voice. She looks at Chris and Dad, then back to me. 'We need to take you to hospital.'

I sip the water and try to stay calm.

Mum's voice is rising, and she's on her feet. 'We need to do something.'

'Come in,' Dad says, pulling out a chair.

I step into the house, breaking all government guidelines, and sit down.

'It's probably just a slight reaction,' I say. 'I don't want to be going to hospital in the middle of a pandemic.'

Mum is on her feet. 'What if it gets worse?'

'I'll be okay.'

'How do you know?'

She turns to Dad. 'What did you put in that tart?'

'Nothing.' He shakes his head.

I cough again and take a deep breath. 'I'll call the NHS number.'

'It's a busy time,' the voice recording tells me. And then gives detailed instructions about what to do if I think I have coronavirus. Eventually it tells me to press one for coronavirus, and two for anything else. I press two and wait.

The operator takes me through some questions. I explain about the Bakewell and lip swelling and throat tightening.

'Based on what you've said, I'm going to call an ambulance,' he says.

'I don't think I'm that bad.' An ambulance seems very dramatic.

'I'll get a nurse to call you back.'

The call comes immediately. 'I understand you've eaten a Bakewell tart?'

'Yes.'

'And had an allergic reaction?'

'Yes.'

'And your lips are swelling and airways tightening?'

'Yes.'

'I'll need to send an ambulance.'

'No, honestly, it's fine. If it gets worse, I can drive to the hospital.'

'But if your airways block on the way, what will you do?'

The thought of being stranded at the side of the road, choking, shocks me into submission.

'I'll send it to your home address,' he says, assuming that I'm following government guidelines.

'I'm not at home.'

'You're not at home?… Where are you?' I hear the accusatory tone in his voice. What he really means is, *Why aren't you at home? You're in tier two, you should be at home.*

'I'm at my parents' house.'

'Right.' On the other end of the phone, he sighs. And loudly.

I am ashamed of myself for coming to my family home and eating Bakewell tart. *I haven't been anywhere or done anything since March*, I want to explain. *We're in a bubble.* But the tightening in my throat is getting worse.

'The ambulance is on its way,' he says.

I hang up and turn to my family. 'I think we're in trouble for coming in.'

'I know we're breaking rules,' Mum says, 'but you couldn't die on the doorstep. What kind of mother do they think I am?'

The ambulance arrives in ten minutes. Two paramedics, a

man and a woman, wearing masks and aprons step into the kitchen. Mum and Dad disappear outside. Chris stands in the doorway.

The paramedics don't tell me off for being in the wrong house; they treat me with kindness.

'So, you've had an allergic reaction to Bakewell tart?' he says.

'I'm not sure if it's the scone or the Bakewell,' I say.

'Do you want another slice while we're here, and we'll find out?' He laughs.

'It's been a day of confectionery,' she says. 'We've just seen a woman who's had four doughnuts.'

'Four!?'

'It's not why she called us out, but, yes, four.'

'That puts my scone and Bakewell slice to shame.'

After doing lots of tests and satisfied that my airways are not going to close, they tell me to call the doctor, who won't see me, but will arrange for me to have an epipen. 'And stay off the scones and Bakewell tarts.'

'I hope it's not the scones,' I say, because scones are an important part of my life. Back in the days when parkruns were permitted, the thought of scones in the café got me up the last hill. I can come to terms with a future without Bakewells in it, but scones… absolutely not.

'Are you okay?' Dad knocks on the door, afraid to step inside.

I nod. 'You tried to kill me!'

'I knew I should have used that Mary Berry recipe.'

21 October 2020

The show must go on

It's Monday evening, almost seven o'clock, when I go upstairs to play my saxophone. On the TV downstairs, the prime minister is briefing the nation about rising coronavirus cases, local lockdowns, and the three-tier system.

I step into my book room and close the door behind me. What the PM failed to realise when he was scheduling his latest briefing is that Monday nights (and Friday afternoons) are for playing the saxophone.

It's how I got through the first lockdown. When all the experts suggested learning a language or playing a musical instrument to pass the time, I dusted down my saxophone, called my music teacher, and started playing (or trying to play) after a break of several years.

During each thirty-minute lesson, and all the rehearsals in between, my mind would empty as I desperately tried to read the music, coordinate fingers and muster enough breath to hit the high notes.

'It's relaxing,' I told Chris after one of my first lessons in lockdown. 'It calms me down.'

He looked at me with a look of desperation. 'It doesn't calm down anyone else,' he said, putting his hands over his ears.

My teacher was much more forgiving. She'd happily encourage me to aim for the high notes, even though there was little hope of reaching them. 'Playing an instrument is good for mindfulness,' she told me. 'It's probably one of the best things you can do.'

For six months, my twice-weekly lessons have lifted my spirits and helped me cope. Now we're facing a second wave and more lockdowns, I need them more than ever.

I prop my phone on the top shelf of the bookcase and wait for my teacher to FaceTime. Downstairs, I hear the prime minister beginning his speech — a feeling of impending doom washes over me. But it doesn't last long because the phone is ringing and my teacher's smiling face pops up on the screen. I smile back.

'How are you?' she asks. 'Have you had a good day?'

'Busy. How about you?'

'I've got some news.' Her voice is high, and she smiles wider.

I lean towards the screen. 'What is it?' I'm keen to get some exciting news, and from the tone in her voice, this definitely sounds exciting.

'I've got a new job.'

'Fantastic!'

'It's in… Spain.'

'Spain! Take me with you!'

She explains how she'd seen the job advert on Friday, applied by the Sunday deadline, received a call on Monday, interviewed Tuesday, had a second interview on Wednesday, and was offered the job on Thursday.

'That's brilliant,' I say, remembering a conversation we'd had during lockdown. I'd been telling her that Barbados was inviting people to work from home over there for a year. 'If only I didn't have dogs and horses and a husband,' I'd told her.

'I'd be straight there.'

And she'd told me about how she and her family would like to move to Spain. Back then, it was just a dream, but now it's happening, and I am happy for her. Delighted that in the middle of a pandemic, with all its sadness, this lovely family are making their dreams come true.

'It's meant to be,' I say, blinking back my tears.

She nods. 'I'll have to find you a new saxophone teacher though.'

'No!' After ten years of my on-off saxophone playing, she's become a friend. Having a new teacher — someone who is not her — is unthinkable. 'I don't want anyone else. We'll do it from Spain. On Zoom, I mean.'

She laughs. 'I might need a few months to get sorted, but we can try. And we'll definitely stay in touch.'

That goes without saying. I fancy a trip to Spain when all this is over.

We chat some more. All our lessons begin with a few minutes of chatting, and then we begin.

'Shall we play one of our old favourites,' she suggests. 'A duet. Maybe give Celine another go?'

Celine Dion's 'My Heart Will Go On' from the film *Titanic*, is our signature piece. We played it together at my wedding a few years ago. It was my first, and probably last, public performance. Trying to negotiate the tricky key change had been one of the most stressful things about the wedding. She'd supported me, and made sure that on the day, I only made a few squeaks.

As Boris Johnson continues to address the nation, we play. I imagine I'm on the *Titanic*, playing as the ship is sinking, chaos all around. It feels rather apt.

I start with a line solo, then in she comes with a solo, then we play together. We've not played it for a long time, but it sounds good. We pause, listening to the instrumental before blasting into the key change, which has not one, not two, not three but four sharps. I take a deep breath, filling my lungs with air. I'm ready. It only takes a few bars in the higher octave for my head to feel light. The room spins.

'I'm fainting.' I throw myself onto an inflatable gym ball that I've been using as a chair, hovering on the edge of consciousness.

'Is Chris there?' she's saying.

I breathe, letting the oxygen into my body. Then I sit up and start laughing.

She laughs too. 'You hear of people passing out and falling on strange objects. Imagine if you'd landed on your saxophone.'

I laugh harder, thinking of the ridiculousness of impaling myself on a musical instrument. We abort the lesson, and I go downstairs, still laughing.

Chris is in front of the TV watching the briefing. 'All I hear when you have your lesson is laughter,' he says.

'It's fun.' I sit next to him and watch the end of the briefing. Even after news of another lockdown, I'm still smiling.

My last saxophone lesson is two weeks later. My teacher has packed up her house in Barnsley and is ready to begin a new life in Spain. We play some of our duets: 'The Lonely Goatherd' from *The Sound of Music*; the Spice Girls' 'Stop'; 'Chasing Pavements'; 'Hit the Road Jack'; and 'Fever'.

'Thank you,' I tell her. 'Our lessons got me through lockdown.'

'It was nice to chat and laugh when all this was happening,' she says.

We say our goodbyes. Lessons are on hold until after Christmas, until a new job, a new home, and a new routine in a new country are established. And are obviously wi-fi dependent.

After she's gone, I stand in my book room, feeling tearful. We've shared so many laughs. Now I'm on my own. I think about putting my saxophone away until January… but that key change still needs some work.

I take a deep breath. She's always been there to count me in. In my head, I hear her. 'And one, two, three, four…' And I'm playing, wobbly at first, but getting stronger. I play my part. I play her part. I even make it through the key change. It's not the same, but, somehow, the show must go on.

24 October 2020

Before you go

I genuinely hope you have enjoyed this book and that it made you smile. I would be hugely grateful if you would leave a review on Amazon. To new authors, like myself, your reviews make a big difference in helping us to promote our books and find new readers.

If you haven't already, you can also sign up to my newsletter, *Life happens, books and cake help*, through my website www.lizchampion.co.uk. You'll get my weekly Slice of Life stories delivered straight into your inbox every Saturday, as well as having the chance to WIN books and get FREE copies of my books before they go on sale. There'll probably be a few servings of cake involved too.

Thank you so much and please keep in touch.

Connect with me on:

Facebook @lizchampionwriter

Twitter @lizchamps

Instagram @lizchampionwriter

Thanks for reading.

Liz x

Acknowledgements

A huge thank you to my friends, family, and readers who have contacted me to say they enjoyed my blog posts. Your support gave me the courage to keep writing, to keep sharing, and put this collection together. Your encouragement means such a lot. I genuinely can't thank you enough.

There are a few wonderful women I'd like to thank for their help in getting my book out into the world. Glenda Strong for her fantastic illustrations. Sarah Gough for her brilliant book cover design. Helena Halme for sharing her publishing knowledge and holding my hand through the publishing process. Dorothy Stannard for editing, and Sue Mitchell, not only for her editing and proofreading, but also her positivity and encouragement over the years. You have all made this book possible, helping me to achieve my dream. I appreciate it so much.

A special thank you to Chris, who is sitting opposite me at the kitchen table as I type, tucking into some left-over chocolate cake. Thank you for being my first reader every Saturday morning. Thank you for believing in me, for always seeing the positives, and for the many laughs. Thank you for everything. I love you.

And finally, the biggest thanks of all goes to my family (Mum, Dad, Sarah and Olivia) — the best cast of characters any writer could wish for. Thank you for letting me write about you, thank you for always being there and for all you do for me. I love you all. And Dad, I hope it's a bestseller so you can order your boat.

Thank you to Glenda Strong

A huge thank you to Glenda Strong for her wonderful illustrations. Glenda does in pictures what I try to do in words (make people smile). It's been a delight to work with her.

About Glenda

Glenda Strong is a Yorkshire based illustrator and artist. She has loved drawing for as long as she could hold a pencil. She also loves birds, Bengal cats, and hot beverages, especially hot chocolate — the really chocolatey kind. She brings ideas to life using pen, paint and a big dollop of humour, telling visual stories to make people smile. Glenda started out her career as an architect where the draughtsmanship she learned taught her the pen control needed to illustrate intuitively. You can find her at www.illustrationsbyglenda.co.uk.

About the Author

Liz Champion is a writer, teacher, and communications special-
ist from Yorkshire. She writes a weekly Slice of Life blog (fuelled
by caffeine and cake) about the highs and lows of everyday life.
As well as writing, she loves books, cake, tea, more books, more
cake, more tea, walking her dogs, running and spending time
with her horses. When she's not doing any of those things,
she'll usually be doing a course — she loves them! So far, she's
gained an MA in creative writing, degrees in English literature,
journalism, and teaching, and grade one saxophone (she's not a
natural). She'd love to hear from you. www.lizchampion.co.uk

You can connect with me on:
- https://lizchampion.co.uk
- https://twitter.com/lizchamps
- https://www.facebook.com/lizchampionwriter

Printed in Great Britain
by Amazon